"THE AIM

of this book is to assemble all that the New Testament tells of the twelve apostles, and to add to that information the most interesting and significant traditions and legends that have come down to us. . . .

"It is my hope and prayer that this book may do something to enable us to value even more highly the twelve men who were in a very special sense the Master's men."

—WILLIAM BARCLAY

The
Master's Men

William Barclay

ABINGDON PRESS
NASHVILLE

THE MASTER'S MEN

A FESTIVAL BOOK

Copyright © 1959 by William Barclay

Published by Jove Publications for Abingdon Press
Festival edition published May 1976
Fourth printing December 1983

ISBN: 0-687-23732-7

Printed in the United States of America

FESTIVAL BOOKS are published by Abingdon Distribution Services, 1015 Visco Drive, Nashville, TN 37210

To J.B.
who also loves stories

PREFACE

This volume began life as a series of articles in the *British Weekly,* and I have to thank Denis Duncan, the editor of that paper, for permission to republish them in this form. In this book the material in these articles has been extensively rewritten; much has been added to it, and not a little has been taken away.

The aim of this book is to assemble all that the New Testament tells of the twelve apostles, and to add to that information the most interesting and significant traditions and legends about them which have come down to us. I am far from claiming that these traditions and legends have any claims to being history; but they have their importance, for the stories which circulate about a man tell us a great deal about that man, even when they are not factually true.

In the nature of things a book like this must be very largely a compilation and can have little in it that is original. The writer of a book like this, therefore, owes many debts. A detailed account of these sources will be found at the end.

It is my hope and prayer that this book may do something to enable us to value even more highly the twelve men who were in a very special sense the Master's men.

WILLIAM BARCLAY

CONTENTS

He that receiveth you receiveth me.

Matt. 10:40

The apostles were made evangelists to us by the Lord Christ. Jesus the Christ was sent by God. Thus Christ is from God, and the apostles from Christ. He and they came into being in harmony from the will of God.

I Clement 42:1-2

We receive both Peter and the other apostles as Christ.

Serapion quoted in Eusebius,
Ecclesiastical History, 6, 12, 3

And the wall of the city had twelve foundations, and in them the names of the twelve apostles of the Lamb.

Rev. 21:14

1

THE TWELVE

In the vision of the writer of the revelation the twelve foundation stones of the wall of the Holy City had inscribed upon them the names of the twelve apostles of the Lamb (Rev. 21:14). The twelve apostles are the foundation stones of the Christian Church. It is, therefore, right that we should study them, not only to learn the facts about them, but also to see what apostleship meant for them and what discipleship must mean for us.

The names of the twelve, or in one case of the eleven, are recorded in four places in the New Testament —Mark 3:16-19; Matt. 10:2-4; Luke 6:14-16; Acts 1:13. Let us set down these four lists side by side as they are given in the King James Version of the Bible.

MARK	MATTHEW
Peter	Peter
James	Andrew
John	James
Andrew	John
Philip	Philip
Batholomew	Bartholomew
Matthew	Thomas
Thomas	Matthew
James, the son of Alphaeus	James, the son of Alphaeus
Thaddeus	Lebbaeus, surnamed Thaddaeus
Simon the Canaanite	Simon the Canaanite
Judas Iscariot	Judas Iscariot

LUKE	ACTS
Peter	Peter
Andrew	James
James	John
John	Andrew
Philip	Philip
Bartholomew	Thomas
Matthew	Bartholomew
Thomas	Matthew
James, the son of Alphaeus	James, the son of Alphaeus
Simon Zelotes	Simon Zelotes
Judas, the brother of James	Judas, the brother of James
Judas Iscariot	

Before we look at the problems of identification which arise from these lists, there are certain minor matters of translation which we must note.

According to the K.J.V., both Mark and Matthew speak of Simon the Canaanite, while Luke speaks of Simon Zēlōtēs, which means Simon the Zealot. In the case of Mark and Matthew the translation of the K.J.V. is in error, an error which was corrected in the English Revised Version and in all subsequent versions. In the best manuscripts of the Greek the word is not *Kananitēs,* which is the word for Canaanite, but *Kananaios.* Simon's descriptive title should be the Cananaean. Cananaean is in fact the Aramaic word for Zēlōtēs. The Cananaeans or Zealots were wild and fanatical nationalists, pledged to harry the Romans by even murder and assassination and by any means, however savage. The word *Kananaios* does not describe Simon's nationality; it describes his political party. Simon was not a Canaanite foreigner; he was a fanatical Jewish nationalist.

In the K.J.V. in Luke and Acts there is a disciple who is called Judas the brother of James. In the Greek

—as the italics of the K.J.V. show—there is no word for brother. The Greek reads simply "Judas of James." This is a very common Greek idiom, and almost invariably it means not brother of, but son of. As the E.R.V. and all subsequent versions have it, this apostle should be described as Judas the son of James. The translation brother instead of son crept in in order to identify this Judas in the apostolic band with the Judas who wrote the letter which we commonly call the Epistle of Jude, and who introduces himself as the brother of James (Jude I).

But these lists present us with a more difficult and a more important problem—a problem in identification. In these lists eleven names are the same; the problem lies in the twelfth name. In Mark the twelfth name is Thaddaeus; in the K.J.V. of Matthew it is "Thaddaeus who was surnamed Lebbaeus"; in Luke and Acts it is "Judas the son of James." We must first note that the explanatory phrase "who was surnamed Lebbaeus" is absent from the great majority of the best manuscripts, and should certainly be omitted, as it is omitted in the E.R.V. How then did this phrase get into the text? There are two possible explanations.

1. Hort suggested that some early scribe did not realize that Matthew and Levi are the same person (Matt. 9:9; Luke 5:27,28); and that Lebbaeus is an attempt to find a place for Levi, or the Levite in the company of the twelve.

2. Thaddaeus is capable of a curious derivation; it could be derived from *thed* which means a breast; such a derivation would indeed provide a strange name for an apostle. On the other hand Lebbaeus could be derived from *leb* which means the heart. It is then suggested that some scribe thought Thaddaeus a very strange name for an apostle, and, as it were, retranslated it into Lebbaeus, which he thought was a more fitting name.

However that may be, if the apostolic company is to be kept to twelve, Thaddaeus and Judas the son of

James must be one and the same person. There is no
real difficulty here. It was not uncommon for a man to
have three names. In Acts 1:23 we read of Joseph,
called Barsabas, who was surnamed Justus. Thaddaeus
may well have had Judas as another of his names, and
when Judas became a name of shame he may well have
dropped it and have become known only as Thaddaeus.
Or, it may well be that Thaddaeus could be the same
name as Theudas, and Theudas could easily become
Judas.

But we have still another problem in identification,
which arises when we add the evidence of the Fourth
Gospel to the evidence of the Synoptic Gospels. In the
Fourth Gospel there is no doubt that Nathanael is one
of the twelve. His call is vividly described in John
1:43-51, and in John 21:2 he is clearly one of the apostolic band. And yet his name does not appear in any
of the lists of the twelve. In this case by far the most
probable solution is that Bartholomew and Nathanael
are one and the same person. Three lines of thought
converge on that conclusion.

1. Nathanael never appears in the Synoptic Gospels,
and equally Bartholomew never appears in the Fourth
Gospel.

2. Bartholomew cannot in any event be a first name.
Bar means son of, and Bartholomew means son of
Tolmai. Bartholomew is in any event a distinguishing
second name, and must have been preceded by another
name.

3. In the Synoptic Gospels Philip and Bartholomew
always appear together; in the lists of Mark, Matthew,
and Luke their names are next to each other. In the
Fourth Gospel it is Philip who finds Nathanael and
who brings him to Jesus (John 1:45). That is to say,
the Synoptic Gospels consistently connect Philip and
Bartholomew, and the Fourth Gospel intimately connects Philip and Nathanael; and, therefore, there is
every probability that Bartholomew and Nathanael are
the same person.

The problems of identification will be solved, if we take Thaddaeus to be the same person as Judas the son of James, and Bartholomew to be the same person as Nathanael.

2

PETER

The Man Who Became a Rock

In every list of the twelve it is Peter who is named first. Peter is the name by which we know best this leader of the apostolic band, but in the New Testament he has three other names as well.

1. When he first appears on the scene he is called Simon (Mark 1:16; John 1:40, 41). That was, so to speak, his own name. Matthew calls him Simon who was called Peter (Matt. 4:18; 10:2). And Simon he remained to the end of the day. There are two kinds of occasions on which Peter is called Simon. He is called Simon on what we might call domestic occasions. Mark and Luke speak of Simon's house and of Simon's wife's mother (Mark 1:29, 30; Luke 4:38). Luke speaks about Simon's fishing boat and Simon's partners in the fishing (Luke 5:3, 10). When Cornelius is directed to Peter it is Simon for whom he is told to inquire (Acts 10:5, 18; 11:13). He is called Simon in the great and intimate moments of his relationship with Jesus. Jesus calls him Simon when he bids him to launch out into the deep (Luke 5:4); in his great commendation at Caesarea Philippi (Matt. 16:17); in his warning that his loyalty would not stand the test (Luke 22:31); in the Garden of Gethsemane when Peter was overpowered by sleep (Mark 14:37). Simon was the name which came most quickly to the lips of those who knew Peter best of all.

2. Twice in the New Testament Peter is called by the name Simeon. He is so-called by James (Acts 15:14), and at the beginning of the second letter which goes by his name (II Pet. 1:1). Simeon is the original

Hebrew form of his name; and Simon is a gentile mod-
ification of Simeon. It was in the church at Jerusalem
that Peter was called Simeon, and it was natural that in
that church the original Hebrew form of his name
should be used.

3. How then did Simon become Peter? It was Jesus
himself who gave Simon his new name (Mark 3:16;
Luke 6:14). It is in John that we have the fullest account of the renaming of Simon. When Andrew
brought his brother Simon to Jesus, Jesus said: "Thou
art Simon the son of Jona: thou shalt be called Cephas,
which is by interpretation, A stone" (John 1:42). As
we shall see, Cephas and Peter are different forms of
the same name. And there is a most interesting point
here. Jona means a dove, and Cephas and Peter mean
a rock. So what Jesus is saying to Peter is: "Up until
now you have been like a fluttering, timorous dove; but
if you take me as Master, and if you give your life to
me, I will make you a rock." In the new name he gave
to him, Jesus put all his hopes and purposes for Peter's
future. In speaking of Peter the gospel writers very frequently put his old and new names together and call
him Simon Peter (Matt. 16:16; Luke 5:8). This is indeed the commonest way in which Peter is referred to
in John (1:40; 6:68; 13:6, 24, 36; 18:10, 15, 25;
20:6; 21:2, 3, 7, 11, 15, 16, 17).

4. We have already said that Peter and Cephas are
the same name. Peter is the Greek and Cephas is the
Aramaic for a rock. In the ancient world nearly everyone spoke Greek, as well as his own native language.
The result was that most people had two names; one
was the Greek name by which he was known in business and in the world, the other was the name by which
he was known in private and to his own friends. So
Thomas is called Didymus; and Thomas is the Aramaic
and Didymus the Greek for a twin. So Tabitha is called
Dorcas, for Tabitha is the Aramaic and Dorcas the
Greek for a gazelle. So in the Highlands of Scotland to
this day Iain is the Gaelic for John and Hamish for

James. Whenever Paul speaks of Peter, he calls him Cephas (I Cor. 1:12; 3:22; 9:5; 15:5; Gal. 2:9). Peter was particularly the apostle to the Jews, and Paul calls him naturally by his Jewish name (Gal. 2:9).

We know more about Peter than about any other of the twelve, and that may well be because of the very close connection between Peter and Mark. So close was the connection that when Peter wrote his own first letter, he could speak of "Marcus my son" (I Pet. 5:13). Peter has the closest possible connection with Mark's gospel. Papias, who was Bishop of Hierapolis in the first half of the second century, was an eager student of how the gospels were written and compiled. He tells us how Mark's gospel came to be written:

> Mark, having become the interpreter of Peter, wrote down accurately everything that he remembered, without however recording in order what was said or done by Christ. For neither did he hear the Lord speak, nor did he follow Him, but afterwards, as I have said, he followed Peter, who adapted his instruction to the needs of his hearers, but had no design of giving a connected account of the Lord's oracles. So then Mark made no mistake while he thus wrote some things down as he remembered them, for he made it his one care not to omit anything that he had heard, or to set down any false statement therein.

From this information we can see that Mark's gospel is nothing other than the preaching material of Peter. It must always stand to the honor of Peter that he kept nothing back. He tells of his own mistakes, of the rebukes he sometimes received from his Master, of his own terrible disloyalty. Peter concealed nothing, for he wished to show the lengths to which the forgiving love and the re-creating grace of Christ had gone for him.

Peter was a fisherman, and it was from the boats and the nets that Jesus called him (Mark 1:16-17.) Peter was a married man (I Cor. 9:5). His home was in Capernaum, and it may well be that Peter's house was Jesus' headquarters when he was in Capernaum, for it was there Jesus went when he came out of the synagogue, and it was there that he healed Peter's wife's mother (Mark 1:29-31; Luke 4:38-39; Matt. 8:14-15).

Peter was a Galilean, and a typical Galilean. Josephus was for a time governor of Galilee and he knew the Galileans well. He says of them: "They were ever fond of innovations, and by nature disposed to changes, and delighted in seditions. . . . They were ever ready to follow a leader and to begin an insurrection." He goes on to say that they were notoriously quick in temper and given to quarreling, but that withal they were the most chivalrous of men. "The Galilaeans have never been destitute of courage" (Josephus, *Life,* 17; *Wars of the Jews,* 3,3,2). The Talmud says of the Galileans: "They were ever more anxious for honour than for gain." Quick-tempered, impulsive, emotional, easily roused by an appeal to adventure, loyal to the end—Peter was a typical man of Galilee.

It was not long before Peter reached the leading place among the twelve. Matthew begins his list of the twelve with the words, "The first, Simon" (Matt. 10:2). The word for first is *prōtos. Prōtos* means first, but it also means chief; and it may well be that Matthew is not merely setting Peter's name first in the list, but that he is saying that Peter was the leader of the apostolic band.

Within the twelve there emerged an inner circle of three who were specially close to Jesus—Peter, James, and John. They were with Jesus at the raising of Jairus' daughter (Mark 5:37; Luke 8:51); on the Mount of Transfiguration (Matt. 17:1; Mark 9:2; Luke 9:28); in the Garden of Gethsemane (Matt. 26:40; Mark 14:37). It was Peter and John who were sent on ahead to prepare for the last Passover in Jerusalem (Luke 22:8).

In the gospel records Peter stands out as the spokesman of the twelve. It was Peter who asked the meaning
of a difficult saying (Matt. 15:15; Luke 12:41). It was
Peter who asked how often he must forgive (Matt.
18:21), and who inquired what was to be the reward
of those who had left all to follow Jesus (Matt.
19:27). It was Peter who asked about the fig tree
which had withered away (Mark 11:21), and about
the meaning of the things which Jesus had said about
the approaching end (Mark 13:3). It was to Peter the
Jews came to ask if Jesus paid his taxes (Matt. 17:24).
It was Peter who answered when Jesus asked who had
touched him in the crowd (Luke 8:45). It was Peter
who asked questions of the risen Christ (John 21:20-
22).

When we study the life of Peter from our New Testament sources we can pick out certain great things in
it.

1. There is the *great discovery*. That discovery has
left its mark both in the Synoptic Gospels and in the
Fourth Gospel. The Fourth Gospel tells how, when
Jesus had fed the five thousand, there was a strong
movement there and then to make him king, and that
he refused to have anything to do with it (John 6:1-
15). The result was that many in disappointment
ceased to follow him. Jesus asked his chosen men if
they too were going to desert him, and thereupon Peter
made his great declaration and his great discovery:
"Lord, to whom shall we go? thou hast the words of
eternal life. And we believe and art sure that thou art
the Christ, the Son of the living God" (John 6:66-69).

The incident in the Synoptic Gospels is even more
vivid and dramatic. For Jesus the time was drawing to
a close, and the forces of the opposition were closing in
upon him. It was essential that he should know if there
was anyone who even dimly realized who he was. He
took his disciples away to the North to Caesarea Philippi for a time of rest and intimate fellowship and
teaching. Then he put the question: "What are men

saying about me?" They told him that some said that
he was John the Baptist, some that he was Elijah, some
that he was Jeremiah, some that he was one of the
prophets. It may have been great, but it was not great
enough. So Jesus put the direct question: "Who do you
say I am?" It was Peter who answered: "Thou art the
Christ, the Son of the living God" (Matt. 16:13-16;
Mark 8:27-29; Luke 9:18-20). Even if there was
nothing else to be said of Peter, he must always remain
the man who was the first to discover who Jesus of Nazareth was.

2. There followed the *great promise*. It was then
that Jesus said to Peter: "Thou art Peter, and upon this
rock I will build my church" (Matt. 16:18). Surely the
meaning of that promise is quite simple. Because Peter
was the first man to discover who Jesus was, because
Peter was the first man to make the confession of faith
which has been the confession of every man who ever
entered the Church, Peter was quite literally the first
member of Christ's Church upon earth, and Peter was,
therefore, the foundation stone of the Church. It must
have been this very saying of which Peter was thinking
when he described his fellow Christians as "lively
stones . . . built up a spiritual house" (I Pet. 2:5).
Every Christian is a living stone in the edifice of the
Church of Christ, and Peter was the first and foundation stone of all.

3. There followed the *great rebuke*. No sooner had
Peter made his great confession than Jesus foretold his
own coming and inevitable death (Matt. 16:21; Mark
8:31; Luke 9:22). Peter was shocked and horrified
and protested that these things must never be; and
Jesus' answer to Peter's protest was, "Get thee behind
me, Satan" (Matt: 16:22-23; Mark 8:32-33). A rebuke so shattering demands explanation. Let us try to
understand it by looking at the matter, first, from
Peter's, and, then, from Jesus' point of view.

Peter's horrified reaction to Jesus' fortelling of his
imminent death came from two causes.

a. It came from love. Peter loved Jesus with all the devotion of his passionate heart. It was unbearable for him to think that Jesus was to end so soon upon a cross.

b. It came from the fact that this announcement of Jesus ran counter to everything that Peter had ever been taught, or knew, or believed. As Matthew has it, Jesus' question was: "Whom do men say that I the Son of man am?" (16:13). Nothing can be more certain than that Jesus habitually used the title Son of man of himself (cf. Luke 7:34; 9:58; 19:10; Mark 10:45). This title was not invented by Jesus. Between the Testaments one of the most influential and popular books was the Book of Enoch. In that book the Son of man is a pre-existent, celestial, supramundane figure waiting in the heavenly places to be unleased to fulfill God's purposes in the world and among men.

This Son of man whom thou hast seen will arouse the kings and mighty ones from their couches and the strong from their thrones, and will loosen the reins of the strong and grind to powder the teeth of sinners. And he will put down the kings from their thrones and kingdoms because they do not extol and praise him, nor thankfully acknowledge whence the kingdom was bestowed upon them. And he will put down the countenance of the strong and shame will cover them: darkness will be their dwelling place and worms their bed, and they will have no hope of rising from their beds because they do not extol the name of the Lord of Spirit. (46:2-5; cf. 48-2-10.)

All his life Peter had been brought up to think of the Son of man as a celestial figure, clad in power and glory, dealing out death and destruction to his enemies. Now Jesus was connecting the Son of man with a cross. Peter's mind was completely incapable of making such a connection.

Peter's reaction to Jesus' foretelling of his sufferings

and death was so violent because his love made such a thought unbearable and the whole background of his thought made it incredible.

Now let us turn to the violence of Jesus' reaction "Get thee behind me, Satan," Jesus said to Peter (Matt. 16:23). The reason for the sternness of Jesus' rebuke was that Peter was presenting him again with the very same temptations as those with which the devil had faced him in the wilderness at the beginning of his ministry (Matt. 4:1-11; Luke 4:1-13). Give them bread—that was the temptation to bid for men's loyalty by the offer of material blessings. Leap off the Temple pinnacle—that was the temptation to dazzle men's eyes with sensations. Fall down and worship me—that was the temptation to compromise with the world's ways. Jesus had been tempted to take the way of power and glory and had deliberately rejected it for the way of the Cross—and in that moment at Caesarea Philippi Peter, out of love, was confronting him with the same temptation again.

4. An even blacker time was to come for Peter, for there was to come the night of the *great denial*. In the Upper Room Peter had affirmed unbreakable loyalty to Jesus (Matt. 26:31-35). In the garden Peter had drawn his sword and had prepared to sell his life dearly for his Master (John 18:10-11). But in the courtyard of the high priest's house Peter's Galilean accent betrayed him, and, when he was challenged with his association with Jesus, he denied that he had ever known him (Mark 14:66-72; Matt. 26:69-75; Luke 22:54-62; John 18:15-27). But certain things must be noted. It is easy to condemn Peter, but the fact is that Peter was in the courtyard of the high priest's house when the other disciples had melted terror-stricken into shadows and fled (Matt. 26:56; Mark 14:50). Peter's failure was the kind of failure that could have happened only to a brave man. He alone was in a position to fail; the others had fled long ago. Again, it must always be remembered that this tragic story of Peter's denial must

go back to none other than Peter himself. If Mark consists of the preaching material of Peter, then one of
Peter's favorite sermons must have been on how he had
failed and how Christ had forgiven.

5. The New Testament history of Peter does not end
there; it goes on to the *great commission*. It is clear
from the gospel story that Peter, after the death of
Jesus, had rejoined the other disciples; and that in itself
was an act of supreme moral courage, because they
must have known well how he had denied their common Lord. It was Peter who was the first to enter the
tomb and to find it empty (John 20:6). It was to Peter
that Jesus sent a special message (Mark 16:7) and
made a special appearance (I Cor. 15:5). No man will
ever know what happened when Peter met his risen
Lord, but Peter must have found "the forgiveness
beyond reason which can meet the sin beyond excuse."
Then by the lakeside there came the day when Peter
was given the commission to be the shepherd of the
flock of Christ (John 21:15-17).

6. Not even yet is the story of Peter ended. There
was still to come the *great realization*. It is clear in the
early chapters of Acts that Peter had become the leader
of the Church. It was Peter who made the first move to
choose another apostle to replace the traitor Judas
(Acts 1:15). It was Peter who was the spokesman of
the Church on the day of Pentecost and who preached
the first Christian sermon (Acts 2:14-40). It was Peter
who, with John, healed the lame man at the beautiful
Gate of the Temple (Acts 3:1-11). It was Peter who
defied the Sanhedrin, when he and John were arrested
for preaching Christ (Acts 4:1-22; 5:26-32). It was
Peter who went to Samaria when the gospel was first
preached there, and who dealt with the deceit of Simon
Magus (Acts 8:12-25). It was Peter who dealt grimly
with the duplicity of Ananias and Sapphira (Acts 5:1-
11). It was Peter who healed Aeneas and Dorcas (Acts
9:32-43).

The greatest step that Peter ever took was the recep-

tion of the gentile Cornelius into the fellowship of the
Christian Church (Acts 10). The Jews were the chosen
people; they despised the gentiles; they could not have
dreamed that the offer of God was made to the gentiles.
It was Peter who realized the universal reach of the
gospel of Jesus Christ, and at the Council of Jerusalem
it was Peter who was instrumental in opening the door
of the Church to the gentiles (Acts 15:7-11). It was
through Peter's action in the case of Cornelius that the
Church experienced the great realization that "God
also to the Gentiles granted repentance unto life" (Acts
11:18).

With this Peter passes from the pages of the New
Testament, and he passes as the great leader of the
Jewish section of the Christian Church. Although the
New Testament itself has no more information about
Peter, many a tradition and many a legend gathered
around his name in the early Church. These legends
connect Peter with three different places.

1. They connect him with Antioch. It is said that
Peter was the first bishop of the church at Antioch, and
that he served that church as bishop for seven years. It
is indeed by no means unlikely that Peter did become
the leader of the church in the city where the gospel
was first preached to the gentiles (Acts 11:20), and
where the Christians were first called Christians (Acts
11:26).

2. They connect him with Asia Minor. It is said that
following upon his time in Antioch Peter preached in
Asia Minor. That also is by no means unlikely, because
his letter is addressed to the Christians who are scat-
tered abroad throughout Pontus, Galatia, Cappadocia,
Asia, and Bithynia (I Pet. 1:1). This first letter of
Peter presents us with something of a problem. It ends
with a greeting from the church that is at Babylon (I
Pet. 5:13). What are we to understand by the word
"Babylon"? There are comparatively few scholars who
would understand the word "Babylon" literally, and yet
B. H. Streeter holds that it is by no means impossible

that Peter actually did preach in Babylon. He argues
that the eyes of a Palestinian Jew would naturally turn
to Babylon. It was the best of the Jews who went into
exile, and many of them never came back. "The purest
stock and the strictest orthodoxy still had its center in
Mesopotamia." At Pentecost the list of those present
begins with those from Parthia, Media, Elam, and Mesopotamia. The Jewish historian Josephus regarded
Babylon as so important that he issued the first edition
of his book on the Jewish wars in Aramaic, specially
for the benefit of his fellow Jews in Babylon and in
Mesopotamia. The greatest exposition of the Jewish
law is the Babylonian Talmud. It is certainly true that
anyone seeking the cream of Jewish scholarship would
turn to Babylon. But there is not even a hint of tradition that Peter ever preached there. Almost unanimously, Babylon is taken to mean Rome. Certainly in
the Revelation Babylon means Rome (14:8; 16:19;
17:5; 18:2). Eusebius, the great early historian, believed that in I Peter Babylon means Rome. "They
say," he writes, "that Peter wrote in Rome itself, as is
indicated by him, when, by a figure, he calls the city
Babylon" (Ecclesiastical History, 2, 15). When the
early Christians thought of the size and might and the
wickedness and the cruelty of Rome, it seemed to them
the exact modern parallel of ancient Babylon, and they
frequently applied that name to it. We may take it as
reasonably certain that Peter did preach in Asia Minor,
but as equally certain that he did not go to Babylon.

3. It is the unanimous tradition of the early Church
that Peter went to Rome, probably about A.D. 61, and
that he was martyred there. There are vivid and interesting legends of Peter in Rome, especially those which
are connected with his death, and which have come
down to us in the apocryphal Acts of Peter. The story
is that in Rome Peter again came into collision with
Simon Magus, with whom he had already dealt in Samaria (Acts 8:9-24). Simon claimed to have raised a
young man from the dead, but Peter showed him up for

the charlatan that he was. Then Simon proposed to
demonstrate his power by flying through the air, but
Peter prayed that his deceit might be demonstrated to
all, and Simon crashed in his attempt and was killed.
Simon had a great following in Rome, and Peter's exposure of him gained him many enemies. Worse was to
follow. By the preaching of Peter the four concubines
of Agrippa, the prefect, were converted and changed
their way of life. Still further, by the influence of Peter,
Xanthippe, the wife of Albinus, the favorite of the Em-
peror, was persuaded to a life of chastity. Both Agrippa
and Albinus were enraged and determined that Peter
must die. Peter was warned and was encouraged by his
friends and by the Christian Church to seek safety in
flight, so that he might be spared yet further to serve
the Lord. But, as Peter was fleeing from the city, he
saw the Lord entering into Rome. "Lord," he said,
"whither goest thou?" (*Domine, quo vadis?*) The Lord
answered: "I go into Rome to be crucified." "Lord,"
said Peter, "art thou being crucified again?" "Yea,
Peter," said the Lord, "I am being crucified again."
(Acts of Peter, 35). Peter understood that Jesus was
going into Rome to bear the cross from which he was
running away. And Peter turned back to die. With a
refinement of cruelty Peter's wife was crucified before
him, while he was compelled to look on. Peter encouraged her, and said: "Remember the Lord" (Eusebius, *Ecclesiastical History*, 3, 30). With such courage
did Peter conduct himself that even his jailer was
moved to accept the Christian faith. When the moment
of crucifixion came Peter requested that he might be
crucified head downwards, for he was not worthy to die
as his Lord had died (*Ecclesiastical History*, 3, 1). In
the end Peter died a martyr and a hero for his Lord.

Peter may have had many faults, but he had always
the saving grace of the loving heart. F. W. Farrar says
of him that his greatest characteristic was that, however
often he might fall and fail, "he always recovered his
courage and his integrity." Luke ends his story of

Peter's denial with a vivid and dramatic sentence: "The Lord turned, and looked upon Peter" (Luke 22:61). One look from the eyes of Jesus could always bring Peter back to the way of honor and fidelity. So we too may pray:

> When Thou see'st me waver
> With a look recall.[1]

[1] James Montgomery, "In the Hour of Trial."

3

JOHN

*The Son of Thunder
Who Became the Apostle of Love*

John was the son of Zebedee and the brother of James. He was a fisherman by trade, and it was while he and his brother James were engaged in mending their nets in the boat by the lakeside with their father that Jesus called them (Matt. 4:21; Mark 1:19). John's connection with Peter was specially close, for Peter was John's partner in the fishing trade (Luke 5:10). We find John going to Peter's house after the Sabbath service in Capernaum (Mark 1:29); and in the last days we find Peter and John being sent out together to prepare the last Passover feast for Jesus and the other disciples (Luke 22:8). As we shall see, in Acts in the early days of the Church, Peter and John were always acting together, and Peter was always the spokesman for the two. They were partners in the fishing boat and they were partners in the task of being fishers of men (Mark 1:17).

It would seem that John, before he became a disciple of Jesus, had been a disciple of John the Baptist. The Fourth Gospel tells of the two disciples of that John who followed Jesus, when he pointed him out as the Lamb of God who takes away the sin of the world. One of these disciples is named as Andrew; the other is not named at all; and the natural conclusion is that the unnamed disciple is John himself (John 1:35-40). Along with Peter and James, John became one of the inner circle of the apostolic band (cf. page 18). John was one of the disciples who was closest to Jesus; it may be he was closest of all.

In the first three Gospels John seldom appears apart from James; for the most part James and John are inseparable, and act and speak as one. From these Gospels there emerges a vivid picture of John—and the strange thing is that it is not an attractive one.

1. John and James emerge as men of ambition. Mark tells how they came to Jesus with the request for the chief places in his kingdom, how the rest of the twelve resented this as an attempt to steal a march upon them, and how Jesus taught them all a much-needed lesson in humility (Mark 10:35-45). When Matthew retells that story he attributes this ambitious request, not to John and James, but to their mother (Matt. 20:20-29). The reason for the change in the story is this. Matthew was writing perhaps thirty years later than Mark. By that time men looked back on the twelve as the princes and foundation stones of the Church, and it was only natural that that which was to their discredit should be removed, or toned down, or explained away. So Matthew attributes the ambitious desire for place and power, not to James and John themselves, but to their mother. But we may well believe that Mark's story is the correct version of what happened.

There may well have been two reasons for this request for the first place in the apostolic band.

a. It may be that James and John were a little better off than the others, and socially a little higher. Certainly their father Zebedee was sufficiently prosperous in business to employ hired servants (Mark 1:20); and James and John may well have felt themselves a cut above the rest.

b. It may be that James and John were closely akin to Jesus. There are three lists of the women who stood by the cross of Jesus at the end. In Mark the list is: Mary Magdalene, Mary the mother of James the Less and of Joses, and Salome (Mark 15:40). In John the list is: Jesus' mother, his mother's sister, Mary the wife of Cleophas, and Mary Magdalene (John 19:25). In

Matthew the list is: Mary Magdalene, Mary the mother
of James and Joses, and the mother of Zebedee's children (Matt. 27:56). Mary Magdalene appears in every
list. Mary the mother James and Joses and Mary the
wife of Cleophas must be identified as the same person.
That being so, the remaining person is called Salome,
the sister of Jesus' mother, and the mother of Zebedee's
children. This would mean that Salome was the mother
of James and John and was a sister of Mary the mother
of Jesus, and that, therefore, James and John were full
cousins of Jesus. It may well be that they thought that
their physical kinship to Jesus gave them a special
claim to a specially favored place in his kingdom.

2. James and John were men of a violent temper.
The direct route from Galilee to Jerusalem necessarily
passes through Samaria, and the Jews had no dealings
with the Samaritans. On his last journey to Jerusalem
Jesus took that route. He sent on messengers ahead to
a Samaritan village to make preparations to stay there;
but the ancient enmity produced the shut door, and
hospitality was discourteously refused. The reaction of
James and John was immediate and violent: "Lord,
wilt thou that we command fire to come down from
heaven, and consume them, even as Elias did?" Jesus
had to remind them that they were followers of one
who had come, not to destroy, but to save (Luke
9:51-56).

It was no doubt for this reason that John and James
received their nickname—Boanerges, the sons of
thunder, as Jesus called them (Mark 3:17). They must
have been violent and explosive characters, with
tempers on a hair trigger and with voices ready to
thunder out in denunciation and condemnation.

3. On only one occasion does John appear alone in
the Synoptic gospels, and he appears as a man of an
intolerant heart. He had seen a man casting out devils
in the name of Jesus. This man was not actually one of
their company, and John had thereupon forbidden him
to carry on the healing work that he was doing (Mark

9:39-40; Luke 9:49-50). Jesus gently told him to let the man be, for he who was not against them was for them.

At first sight John appears as a man of overreaching ambition, a man with an explosive temper, a man of an intolerant heart.

I believe that there is something to add to his story and this picture. As we have seen, John appears frequently in the story of the Synoptic Gospels, but never once does he appear by name in the Fourth Gospel. But in the Fourth Gospel there appears a character who is called The Beloved Disciple. In ancient times no one doubted that the Beloved Disciple was John.[1] But in modern times the identification of the Beloved Disciple with John has been widely disputed.

As a matter of interest we may briefly note certain of the main theories which have been advanced.

1. It has been suggested that the Beloved Disciple is not an actual historical person at all, but that he is an ideal figure, "the exquisite creation of a devout imagination."

2. Strange as it may seem, the Beloved Disciple has been identified with Judas Iscariot. It is claimed that only Judas understood the mind of Jesus, and that the action of Judas was a deliberate aiding of Jesus to do the task which had been given him to do. There was, indeed, a Gnostic sect who had a gospel according to Judas, and who saw in Judas the ideal Gnostic who alone of all men had understood Christ and had helped him to die. The identification of Judas and the Beloved Disciple is rendered impossible by the narrative of John 13:21-30 where the two characters are obviously different.

3. The Beloved Disciple has been identified with Nathanael, the Israelite in whom there was no guile

---

[1] Cf. Irenaeus, *Against Heresies*, 3, 1, 1; Eusibius, *Ecclesiastical History*, 6, 25.

(John 1:43-51), and who was clearly near and dear to the heart of Jesus.

4. The Beloved Disciple has been identified with the young man of Mark 14:51, who was present at the arrest, and who fled naked, leaving his linen sheet in the hands of the soldiers.

5. The Beloved Disciple has been identified with Lazarus, for in the Lazarus story it is three times said that Jesus loved Lazarus (John 11:3, 5, 36).

6. The Beloved Disciple has been identified with the rich young ruler. In Mark's story it is said that Jesus "beholding him loved him" (Mark 10:21). A romantic story is built up in which the rich young ruler later gave his heart to Jesus, and afterwards became the "good man of the house" who gave Jesus and his disciples the room for the Passover feast (Mark 14:14). It is conjectured that he was present at the Last Supper and was the Beloved Disciple on whose breast Jesus leaned.

The great argument which is used against identifying the apostle John with the Beloved Disciple is the difference in their characters. John is the ambitious, angry, intolerant character; the Beloved Disciple is the figure of love. But I believe that the traditional view is correct—that the apostle John and the Beloved Disciple are one and the same, and that the very point of John's whole life is the change which Jesus Christ wrought in him, whereby the son of thunder did become the apostle of love.

Let us then see what the New Testament has to say about the Beloved Disciple. At an ancient feast people reclined on low couches with the feet stretched out behind, leaning on the left arm, thus leaving the right hand free to deal with the food. At the Last Supper the Beloved Disciple leaned on Jesus' breast, which means that he must have been sitting at Jesus' right hand. It was to him that Peter signed to ask who the traitor was (John 13:21-25). It was to the care of the Beloved Disciple that Jesus entrusted Mary his Mother (John 19:26,27). It was the Beloved Disciple who arrived

first at the tomb on Easter morning (John 20:1-10).
The Beloved Disciple was there at the lakeside when
Jesus appeared to his men; it was about his future that
Peter asked, only to be rebuked; and it is there that it is
said that his authority lies behind the gospel which
bears the name of John (ch. 21).

Before we leave the New Testament it may be that
we can add still a little more about John. In John
18:15, 16 another unnamed disciple appears in the
gospel narrative. When Jesus was arrested, Peter and
this unnamed disciple followed to see what would happen; and they were able to gain an entry to the courtyard of the high priest's house, because this unnamed
disciple was known to the high priest. John's acquaint-
ance with the high priest may be explained in one of
two ways.

1. There is extant a letter written by Polycrates who
was Bishop of Ephesus about A.D. 190. In it he describes John as "a witness and a teacher, who reclined
upon the bosom of the Lord, and who was a priest and
wore the priestly diadem" (Eusebius, *Ecclesiastical
History*, 3, 31). If Polycrates is right, then John had
high-priestly connections, and entrance to the high
priest's house would be easy.

2. It may be that the second explanation is the more
probable. H. V. Morton in *In the Steps of the Master*
gives us some very interesting information:

There is in the back streets of Jerusalem a dark little
hovel, now, I believe, an Arab coffee-house, which
contains stones and arches, that were once part of an
early Christian Church. The Franciscan tradition is that
this Church was erected on the site of a house which
had belonged to Zebedee, the father of St. John. This
family, said the Franciscan, were fish merchants of Galilee, with a branch office in Jerusalem, from which
they used to supply, among others, the family of the
High Priest.

This would explain how John was known to the door-keeper of the high priest's house, and it would also explain how Zebedee's fishing business was prosperous enough to enable him to employ hired servants in addition to his sons (Mark 1:20).

So we come to the end of the gospel evidence which leaves us with the picture of a man of a tempestuous nature who under the hand of Jesus became a man of love.

In Acts John is still prominent in the story, but he never speaks. Always he is found in the company of Peter, and it is always Peter who is spokesman for both. John is there when the lame man is healed at the Beautiful Gate of the Temple (Acts 3:1-10). He was with Peter when they were both imprisoned, and when Peter made his courageous speech before the Sanhedrin (*Acts* 4:1-22). He went with Peter to Samaria to see the amazing results of the preaching of Philip (Acts 8:14). Paul names him as one of the great leaders of the Christian Church (Gal. 2:9).

With this John passes from the pages of the New Testament; and for further information about him we must move into the realm of legend and tradition. Many of the later stories about John are obviously works of pious fiction and imagination, but there are others which ring true, and from them there emerges a picture of John which is closely consistent with what the writings of the New Testament tell us about him.

John, it is said, was faithful to the trust which Jesus reposed in him when he committed Mary to his charge (John 19:26-27). John stayed in Jerusalem and cared for Mary like a son until the day of her death (Nicephorus, *The Ecclesiastical History,* 2, 2). Perhaps it was after the death of Mary that John found his way to Rome. There he came under persecution. He was flung into a cauldron of boiling oil (Tertullian, *De Praescriptione,* 36), but emerged unharmed. Later tradition in Jerome added the further embroidery to the tale that he emerged purer and fresher than when he was thrown

in! He was compelled to drink the cup of hemlock, but
it did him no harm.

It is the consistent tradition of the early Church that
thereafter John was banished to the island of Patmos,
most probably in the time of Domitian (Irenaeus,
Against Heresies, 5, 30, 3; Eusebius, *The Ecclesiastical
History,* 3, 18, 1; Jerome, *On Illustrious Men,* 9). On
being liberated from Patmos, he came to Ephesus, and
there he became a leading figure with a unique position
in the Church. It is at this period of his life that the
traditions gather around him—and they are characteristic of him.

In Ephesus there was an archheretic called
Cerinthus. He was a Docetist; that is to say he taught
that Jesus never had a flesh and blood body but was
only a phantom walking in the appearance of a man.
Such a belief was destructive of the whole Christian
faith, and it was anathema to anyone who believed that
the Word was made flesh (John 1:14; cf. I John 4:3).
Irenaeus tells us that one day John was going to bathe
in the bathhouse in Ephesus when he learned that
Cerinthus was already in it. "Let us flee," he ex-
claimed, "lest even the bathhouse fall down, because
Cerinthus the enemy of truth is therein" (*Against
Heresies,* 3, 3, 4). The fire of the old days never died
in John's heart.

The second story of the days in Ephesus is passed
down to us by Clement of Alexandria. Once in visiting
a certain congregation John saw within it a most handsome young man "of refined appearance and of ardent
spirit." Pointing at the youth, John said to the bishop
of the congregation, "This man I entrust to your care
with all earnestness in the presence of the church and
of Christ as witnesses." The bishop accepted the trust
and pledged himself to it. He took the youth into his
own home, cherished him, taught him, and finally baptized him. Then he relaxed his care and vigilance—too
soon. The youth fell into evil company who seduced

him into dissolute luxury and taught him to be a robber.

The young man grew accustomed to this new kind of life. "Like a restive and powerful horse which starts aside from the right path and takes the bit between its teeth, he rushed all the more violently because of his great nature towards the pit." The youth himself decided that he had drifted beyond the mercy of God, and he organized a robber band of which he became chief, "the most violent, the most blood-thirsty, the most cruel."

There came the day when John revisited the church in which he had first seen the youth. He said to the bishop, "Now, bishop, return to us the deposit which Christ and I entrusted to your care in the presence and with the witness of the church over which you preside." The bishop was amazed, thinking at first that it was some entrusted money that John was talking about. "It is the youth," said John, "and the soul of our brother that I demand back." With sorrow in his voice, the bishop answered, "The man is dead." "By what death did he die?" demanded John. "He is dead to God," said the bishop, and went on to tell how the youth had slipped from grace, and had become a robber chieftain. John rent his clothes. "A fine guardian of our brother's soul it was that I left!" he said.

John called for a horse and a guide and rode straight from the church to find the youth. When he came near to the headquarters of the robber band he was captured by the robber's sentries. He made no effort to escape. "It was for this very purpose that I came," he said. "Take me to your leader." So he was brought to the leader, who was waiting fully armed, but when he recognized John, he was smitten with shame and turned and fled from his presence. Forgetting his old age, John pursued him. "Why do you flee from me, my child," he said, "from your own father, from me a poor, old, unarmed man? Have pity upon me, and do not fear. You have still hope of life. I myself will give account to

Christ for you. If need be, I will willingly undergo your
penalty of death, as the Lord did for us. I will give my
own life in payment for yours. Stand! Believe! Christ
has sent me!" On hearing this the youth threw away his
weapons and fell to trembling and to tears. With bitter
contrition he repented, and John assured him that he
had found pardon with his Saviour for him. He prayed
with him; he brought him back to the church; he never
ceased to keep his grip upon him; and in the end the
young man was so changed by Christ that he became
the bishop of the congregation (Clement of Alexandria,
The Rich Man's Salvation, 42).

Surely there never was a more characteristic story of
John, for in it the old anger is used to the glory of
Christ by the new love.

There are two further fragments of tradition which
have something to add to the picture. The one is handed down by John Cassian, and must be quoted in full:

> It is said that the blessed John while he was gently
> stroking a partridge with his hands, suddenly saw a
> philosopher approaching him, in the dress of a hunt-
> er. The philosopher was astonished that a man of
> such great fame and reputation should demean him-
> self to such paltry and trivial amusements, and said:
> "Can you be that John whose great and famous rep-
> utation attracted me also with the greatest desire for
> your acquaintance? Why then do you occupy your-
> self with such poor amusements?" John answered
> him: "What is that that you are carrying in your
> hand?" "A bow," answered the other. "And why,"
> said John, "do you not carry it everywhere bent?"
> The other answered: "That would not do, for the
> force of its stiffness would be relaxed, if it were con-
> tinually bent, it would be lessened and destroyed,
> and when the time came for it to send stouter arrows
> after some beast, its stiffness would be lost by the
> excessive and continuous strain, and it would be im-
> possible for the more powerful bolts to be shot."

"So, my lad," said John, "do not let this slight and
short relaxation of my mind disturb you, as, unless it
sometimes relieved and relaxed the rigour of its purpose by some recreation, the spirit would lose spring
owing to the unbroken strain, and would be unable
when need required, implicitly to follow what was
right." (*Conferences,* 24, 21.)

"The bow that is bent will soon cease to shoot straight"
—that, too, may well have been something which the
intense nature of John learned in the mellowing of age.

There is one other fragment of tradition which
Jerome has handed down to us.

When John tarried in Ephesus to extreme old age,
and could only with difficulty be carried to the
church in the arms of his disciples, and was unable
to give utterance to many words, he used to say no
more at their several meetings than this: "Little
children, love one another." At length the disciples
and fathers who were there, wearied with always
hearing the same words, said: "Master, why dost
thou always say this?" "It is the Lord's command,"
was his reply, "and, if this alone be done, it is
enough." (*Commentary on Galatians,* 6, 10.)

In the end John had forgotten everything except his
Lord's command of love.

In the end, they say, he was buried, but even in the
grave he was still alive. It was said, says Augustine,
that "he showed that he was still alive by the movement
of the dust above, which was stirred by the breath of
the saint." And Augustine piously adds: "I think it
needless to contest the opinion. Those who know the
place must see whether the soil is so affected as it is
said; since I have heard the story from men not unworthy of credence." (*Tractates on John,* 124, 2.)

John is the supreme example of how Jesus Christ
can take a man as he is and use his natural gifts and

powers and temperament for greatness. Power itself is always neutral. Power becomes good or bad according to the mind and heart of the person by whom it is controlled and used. In John there was always power, and the power was united with loveliness when it was controlled by Jesus Christ.

4

ANDREW

The Man Who Introduced Others to Jesus

Andrew has the very unusual distinction of being the patron saint of no fewer than three different countries —Russia, Greece, and Scotland. There is not very much direct information about Andrew in the New Testament, but the information which the gospel story does contain is such that it paints an unmistakable picture of the kind of man that Andrew was.

Andrew was a native of Bethsaida (John 1:44). He was a fisherman by trade, and it was when he was plying his trade and mending his nets that Jesus called him to be a fisher of men (Mark 1:16-18; Matt. 4:18-20).

Andrew began by being a follower and disciple of John the Baptist, and, according to John's telling of the story, Andrew was the first of all the twelve to attach himself to Jesus, along with John. It was on the day when John the Baptist first pointed out Jesus as the Lamb of God who takes away the sin of the world that Andrew and John made their first contact with Jesus (John 1:35-39). In the early Church Andrew is frequently called by the title *Prōtoklētos,* which literally means First-called.

No sooner did Andrew discover Jesus for himself than he went to find his brother Peter to bring him to Jesus. Andrew and Peter lived together (Mark 1:29); no doubt all their lives they had shared everything, and now Andrew wished to share with his brother the greatest discovery that he had ever made.

It is here that the greatness of Andrew begins to emerge. It was not long before Peter had acquired an undisputed leadership in the apostolic band, and in that

band Peter, James, and John formed an inner circle
who were with Jesus in the greatest and the most intimate moments. Andrew was never in that inner circle,
although sometimes he must have been on the fringe of
it, as on the occasion when with the inner three he
shared in asking Jesus questions about the things to
come (Mark 13:3). There was something even more
than that. Andrew is regularly described and identified
as Simon Peter's brother. He is so called in the list of
the twelve in both Matthew and Luke (Matt. 10:2;
Luke 6:14), and in the incident of the feeding of the
five thousand when he brought the lad to Jesus (John
6:8). The inference is that people might not know who
Andrew was, but everyone knew who Peter was, and
the best way to identify Andrew was to call him the
brother of the famous and outstanding Peter.

There are very few people in Andrew's position who
could have borne that situation with graciousness and
without resentment. Was Andrew not one of the first
two disciples to attach themselves to Jesus? Yet he was
not one of the inner circle, although John was. Was it
not Andrew who brought Peter to Jesus? Yet it was
Peter who had the pre-eminence, and Andrew was
only his brother. Andrew must have been one of those
rare people who are prepared to take the second place.
Even in the Church there are people who grudge others
the place and the prominence that they believe they
ought to have. But Andrew was one of those people
who did not care who received the first place. All he
wanted was to be near to Jesus. So long as the work
was done, it was a matter of no importance to Andrew
who received the credit for doing it. Andrew was the
kind of man who never received the first place; yet he
was also the kind of man on whom every leader de-
pends, and who is the backbone of the Christian
Church and the salt of the earth.

In the first three Gospels there is no mention of Andrew other than in the lists of the twelve. It is in the
Fourth Gospel that Andrew appears as a person and

acquires a personality. On three occasions Andrew emerges from the background, and on every one of these three occasions Andrew is introducing someone else to Jesus.

1. Andrew began by introducing his brother Peter to Jesus (John 1:40-42). For Andrew missionary work began at home. It still often happens that he who is looking for something to do for Jesus Christ will find it in his own home. It is unhappily true that the members of the family of a man who is engaged in church work and service are strangers to the Church. In seeking a task to do for Christ it can also be true that "the eyes of a fool are in the ends of the earth" (Prov. 17:24).

2. On the second occasion on which we meet Andrew he is bringing to Jesus the lad with the five loaves and the two fishes (John 6:8-9). Andrew was eager to bring to Christ anyone who could possibly be of use to Jesus, even if he felt that there was little that could be done.

3. On the third occasion on which we meet Andrew he was bringing the Greeks to Jesus (John 12:20-22). The Greeks had come to Philip with the request to see Jesus. Philip did not know what to do with them. He consulted Andrew, and Andrew had no doubt that they must be brought to Jesus. Whatever else is true of Andrew, it is true of him that he understood Jesus so well that he knew that there was no one whom Jesus did not wish to see, and that there was no time when Jesus was too busy to give himself to the seeking and the inquiring searcher for the truth.

When we consider these three occasions on which Andrew is depicted as bringing people to Jesus, we may say three things about Andrew in his seeking to bring others to Christ.

1. Andrew sought *selflessly*. Andrew could not have lived with Peter all his life for nothing. He knew that Peter was a natural and instinctive leader; he knew that when Peter was there other people must take a back seat. But that did not matter to Andrew. He sought to

bring others to Jesus, even if the bringing of them
meant the inevitable loss of his own pre-eminence.

2. He sought *optimistically*. It was certainly opti-
mistic to think that the lad with his five loaves and two
fishes could do anything to help to feed the five thousand. But Andrew at least hoped that Jesus could use
greatly any gifts which anyone could bring to him. It
never struck Andrew that anyone could be useless to
Jesus.

3. He sought *universally*. It was unnatural for a Jew
to think that anyone of another race could possibly be
of any use to God. To the rigid Jew the gentiles were
accursed. But Andrew was one of the first—perhaps
the very first—to see the universality of the gospel, and
to feel instinctively that Jesus had a message and a
welcome for all mankind.

George Milligan in his article on Andrew in *The
Dictionary of Christ and the Gospels* makes the interesting point that Andrew was at one and the same time
the first home missionary and the first foreign missionary. He was a home missionary when he brought Peter
and the lad to Jesus; he was a foreign missionary when
he brought the Greeks to Jesus. That is indeed a claim
to fame.

With these incidents the information about Andrew
in the New Testament comes to an end; but legend and
tradition wove many a story round his name. As we
began by saying, Andrew became connected with three
different countries.

1. Tradition makes Andrew a preacher in many
lands—in Cappadocia, in Bithynia, in Galatia, and in
Byzantium. But Andrew was specially connected with
Scythia (Eusebius, *Ecclesiastical History,* 3, 1, 1). In
the ancient world the Scythians were a synonym for the
depths of barbarity. Bengel describes them as "more
barbarous than the barbarians." Josephus says that
"They were little different from wild beasts" (*Against
Apion,* 2, 37). T. K. Abbott says that in the ancient
world the word "Scythian" was used as modern custom

uses the word "Goth" for any rough, uncouth, and savage person. So tradition says that Andrew brought the barbarous Scythians also to Jesus.

Scythia was the country north of the Black Sea and between the River Danube and the River Tanais. That is to say, it corresponded in part to modern Russia, and that is why Andrew became known as the patron saint of Russia.

2. According to tradition it was in Achaia in Greece in the town of Patras that Andrew died a martyr. When Andrew came to Patras, so the story runs, Iphidamia, who was already a Christian, told him that Maximilla, the wife of Aegeas, the governor, was on the point of death. Aegeas was standing, sword in hand, ready to kill himself when his wife should die. Andrew miraculously healed Maximilla, who became a Christian, although Aegeas remained hostile to the Christian faith. Aegeas had a brother called Stratocles, whose favorite servant Alcman was dangerously and painfully ill. He too was cured by Andrew, and Stratocles also became a Christian. Aegeas was enraged by the conversion of his wife and his brother and arrested Andrew. In due time Andrew was condemned. In order to prolong his agony he was not nailed but only bound to the cross, to be left to die of hunger and thirst and exposure. When he was faced with the cross Andrew prayed, and part of one version of his prayer runs as follows:

Hail, precious cross! Thou hast been consecrated by the body of my Lord, and adorned with his limbs as rich jewels. I come to thee exulting and glad. Receive me with joy into thy arms. O good cross, thou hast received beauty from our Lord's limbs. I have ardently loved thee. Long have I desired and sought thee. Now thou art found by me, and art made ready for my longing soul. Receive me into thine arms; take me up from among men, and present me to my Master, that he who redeemed me on thee may receive me by thee.

So, they say, that Andrew was scourged with rods by
seven lictors, fastened to his cross, and left to die. It is
a later addition to the story that Andrew asked to be
crucified on the X-shaped cross, which is still called
the St. Andrew's cross, because he was unworthy to die
on the same kind of cross of his Lord. Even if we
doubt the details, we cannot doubt that Andrew died a
martyr for his Master. It was because he was martyred
in Patras in Achaia that Andrew became the patron
saint of Greece.

3. The third country with which Andrew is connected is Scotland. The legend which connects Andrew
with Scotland is late, but for any Scot it must be of
very great interest. It is said that in A.D. 337 Constan-
tine brought Andrew's coffin to Byzantium or Constan-
tinople. Some time in the eighth century a monk called
Regulus was told by an angel to take with him from
Andrew's relics three fingers of the right hand, an arm-
bone, one tooth, and a kneecap, and to travel to the
west with them. He did so, and traveled far, until finally he reached the east coast of Scotland at the place
where St. Andrews now stands. There he settled and
became, according to the story, the first Bishop of St.
Andrews, and the ruins of St. Regulus' Church still
stand there.

Hungus, who was king of the Picts at that time, was
at war with Athelstan, king of the English. On the eve
of the battle Andrew appeared to Hungus in a dream
and assured him of victory. So the old legend goes on:
"And on the morrow a shining cross was seen in the
sky straight above the army of the Picts, not unlike the
same cross that the apostle died on. This cross vanished never out of the sky, till the victory succeeded to
the Picts." The Picts advanced to the battle with the
battle cry, "St. Andrew, our patron, be our guide!"
They utterly defeated the English "who had been terri-
fied seeing the cross shine with awful beams in the
sky." So, they say, that ever afterwards the white St.

Andrew's cross on the blue background of the sky became the standard of Scotland.

There is something very attractive about Andrew. Life placed him in a position where it would have been easy for him to grow resentful and embittered, but he was well content with the second place, because his one endeavor was to serve Jesus Christ, and not to glorify himself. All his life he brought men to Jesus, and he died engaged on that same task. Andrew lived and died a missionary of Christ.

5

THOMAS

The Man Who Became Certain by Doubting

Popular proverbial language has dealt unkindly with Thomas, for Thomas is commemorated in the phrase "a doubting Thomas." No doubt there is an element of truth in that phrase, but there is also something very like a slander.

The first three Gospels tell us nothing about Thomas except his name; it is in the Fourth Gospel that Thomas becomes a clearly defined and vivid character.

In the Fourth Gospel Thomas is usually referred to as "Thomas who is called Didymus." Thomas is the Hebrew, and Didymus is the Greek for a twin. The most startling interpretation of that name is in the Acts of Thomas. In that book Thomas is regularly called Judas. That Thomas would have another name is certain. In the ancient world there were no surnames. As is the case today, certain first names were very common, and it was necessary to add to them some distinguishing second name. Thomas, or Didymus, is clearly a distinguishing second name; and Thomas's full name may very well have been Judas the Twin. In the gospel story there is a Judah or Judas who in Mark 6:3 and Matt. 13:55 is referred to as a brother of Jesus; and the apocryphal Acts of Thomas declare that Thomas was none other than the twin brother of Jesus himself (Acts of Thomas, 31). That is, to say the least of it, most unlikely to be true. But it is nonetheless significant, for the fact that such a tradition could arise is the proof that men felt that Thomas and Jesus were very close together.

In the Fourth Gospel Thomas emerges as a man of certain very definite characteristics.

1. Thomas was the man of courage. Thomas first appears in the Lazarus story (John 11:1-16). News had come that Lazarus was ill, and for two days Jesus made no move at all. Then he prepared to go to Bethany. Bethany was very close to Jerusalem; it was indeed one of the villages in which pilgrims to the Passover normally lodged. By this time the Jewish authorities in Jerusalem were determined that Jesus should die, and on two occasions he had been in danger of being stoned to death (John 8:59; 10:31). To go to Jerusalem seemed a suicidal act of recklessness. What made it worse was that news had come that Lazarus was dead and to go to Jerusalem now seemed not only reckless, but also useless. When Jesus intimated his intention to go to Jerusalem, the disciples came very near to abandoning him. Then there came the voice of the normally silent Thomas, "Let us also go, that we may die with him" (John 11:16). Ahead Thomas could see nothing but disaster, but nevertheless he was for going on. Thomas was grimly determined to be faithful unto death.

It is easy for an optimist to be loyal in a difficult situation, for an optimist always expects the best. It is much harder for a pessimist to be loyal in such a situation, for a pessimist always expects the worst. Thomas was constitutionally a pessimist. He could see nothing but disaster ahead, but for him that was no reason for turning back. For Thomas there might be death, but there could never be disloyalty. It may well be that it was Thomas who rallied the faltering loyalty of the other eleven, on that day when Jesus announced his intention of going to Jerusalem.

2. Thomas was the man who was bewildered. It is clear that in those days toward the end Thomas lived in a bleak bewilderment. In the Upper Room Jesus was seeking to persuade the dull minds of the disciples to see the Cross, and to see what lay beyond the cross.

"Whither I go you know," he said, "and the way you know." Thomas broke in, "Lord, we know not whither thou goest; and how can we know the way?" Thomas received the great answer from Jesus, "I am the way, the truth, and the life" (John 14:1-6).

Thomas was a man who could not live with an unasked question. It has been said that the whole art of gaining and of communicating knowledge consists in asking the right questions. It could be said that the way to certainty is to have the right kind of doubt.

The answer of Jesus to Thomas is clear. Jesus was saying to him: "Thomas, I know that you do not understand what is happening. No one understands. But whatever happens, *you have got me*. I am the way, the truth, and the life." In this world, in the last analysis, what we need is not an argument but a presence. No argument is convincing, and what Jesus offers us is not an argument, but himself.

3. Thomas was the man who could not believe. When Jesus had died upon the cross, and when it seemed that the end had finally come, Thomas' only desire was to be alone. When a well-bred animal is injured, it creeps away to suffer alone, and there was something like that about Thomas. So it happened that when Jesus came back to the disciples Thomas was not there, and he utterly refused to believe the good news. He said that he would not believe unless he actually saw and touched and handled the nailprints in Jesus' hands and the gash of the spear in his side (John 20:25). Thomas had to see for himself before he would believe.

4. Thomas became the man of devotion and of faith. Jesus came back. He invited Thomas to put his finger in the nailprints and his hand in his side. Confronted with the risen Lord, Thomas breathed out the greatest confession of faith in the New Testament: "My Lord, and My God" (John 20:26-28). Thomas' long doubt was turned to certainty in the presence of his Lord.

Two outstanding facts emerge from the story of Thomas in the New Testament.

The first truth is that *Jesus blames no man for wanting to be sure.* Jesus did not blame Thomas for his doubts; Jesus knew that once Thomas had fought his way through the wilderness of his doubts he would be the surest man in Christendom. Jesus never says to a man, "You must have no doubts." Rather he says, "You must never profess a faith of which you are not absolutely sure, and you must fight your battle until you reach your certainty." But it must be noted that certainty came to Thomas, not through intellectual conviction of the truth of a creed, but through firsthand experience of the power and the presence of Jesus Christ. Thomas became sure, not of things about Jesus Christ, but of Jesus Christ himself.

The second truth is that *certainty is most likely to come to a man in the fellowship of believers.* When Thomas was alone he was doubly alone. By cutting himself off from the fellowship of men he had also cut himself off from the fellowship of Jesus Christ, and it was when he came back into that fellowship that he met Christ again. That is not to say that a man cannot find Jesus Christ in the solitude and the silence, but it is to say that nowhere is a man more likely to find Christ than in the company of those who love Christ.

The Fourth Gospel gives us one more glimpse of Thomas, for Thomas was there when Jesus came back to meet his men beside the Sea of Galilee (John 21:2). Thomas had learned his lesson; from now on he was one with the fellowship of believers, and he was there when Jesus Christ came to his own.

The New Testament has no more to tell us about Thomas, but legend and tradition have much to say of him. There are two streams of tradition about Thomas.

The first says that Thomas worked in Parthia. Eusebius passes down the information that when the disciples portioned out their different spheres "Parthia was allotted to Thomas," and Socrates repeats this story

(Eusebius, *Ecclesiastical History,* 3, 1; Socrates, *Ecclesiastical History,* 1, 19). Both Socrates and Sozomen speak of a magnificent memorial church to Thomas and to his martyrdom in Edessa in Mesopotamia (Socrates, *Ecclesiastical History,* 4, 18; Sozomen, *Ecclesiastical History,* 6, 18). At that time Parthia was an independent kingdom stretching from the Indus to the Tigris, and from the Persian Gulf to the Caspian Sea. The Parthians were a stubbornly independent race whom even the Romans respected and feared, and there is a steady tradition that Thomas preached among them.

The second stream of tradition is much more detailed and, therefore, much more interesting. Sophronius, in his additions to Jerome's *Lives of Illustrious Men,* says that Thomas preached the gospel "to the Parthians, Medes, Persians, Carmanians, Hyrcanians, Bactrians and Magians and died at Calamina in India." So the second stream of tradition connects Thomas with India. It is quite true that in the ancient world the term India was used vaguely and loosely. India was not uncommonly used as a designation of the countries about the south of the Red Sea and the Persian Gulf— countries such as Abyssinia, Southern Arabia, and Southern Persia.

To this day in South India there is a church which call itself "The Christians of St. Thomas," and which traces its descent and its origin direct to the apostle Thomas. The origin of that church is wrapped in mystery. When Vasco da Gama and his Portuguese explorers arrived in India round about A.D. 1500 they found that church already there. It flourished in Malabar and Travancore. Its own account of its origin was that Thomas had landed at Malankara, an island of the lagoon near Crangamore, and that he had preached to the natives and baptized many converts. He was said to have ordained seven priests and founded two churches. It was said that thereafter he had moved across to Mailapore (Myalapur), which is now a suburb of Madras, and that there he had converted the king and all the people. The story goes on to say that Thomas had moved on to China and that he had had equal success there. After his work in China he returned to Maila-pore, where the Brahmins grew jealous of his success. They incited the people to stone him, and finally he was killed by the thrust of a lance. Vasco da Gama and his men discovered many Christian relics there. In particular they found a Christian chapel, and digging under it they unearthed human bones of such dazzling whiteness that they concluded that they must be those of none other than Thomas himself!

As we have said, the coming of Christianity to India is wrapped in mystery, but it certainly goes very far back. On St. Thomas' Mount at Mailapore a stone cross was discovered. It has on it an inscription in the Pahlavi language:

In punishment by the Cross was the suffering of this One;
He who is the true Christ, the God alone, the Guide ever pure.

That cross dates back most probably to the eighth century, and a companion to it was found in Kottayam in Travancore, in this case dating back to the tenth century.

We get other glimpses of Christianity in India. At the Nicene Council one of the signatories was John of Persia, Bishop of all Persia and of Great India, in truth a vast diocese, whatever India means in the title. *The Anglo-Saxon Chronicle* tells that Sighelm and Athelstan were sent by King Alfred with alms to Rome and thence to India to Thomas and Bartholomew. But the most valuable evidence comes from *The Universal Christian Topography* written by Cosmas Indicopleustes, who in the early sixth century made a voyage to India. He tells us that he found Christians and a church "in Malabar, the land where the pepper grows,"

and in Caliana, south of Bombay, a bishop who took
his appointment from Persia. This is positive proof that
there were Christians in India in A.D. 500.

It so happens that one of the most interesting apocryphal books of acts is the Acts of Thomas, and its
story is the story of how Thomas was sent to India, and
of how he worked there. Its story runs as follows.

A day came when the apostles met in Jerusalem, re-
membering Christ's command that they must be his
witnesses even unto the uttermost part of the earth
(Acts 1:8). So they divided up the world between
them and decided by lot where each of them should go.
To Thomas the work in India fell, and Thomas would
not go. He said that he was not strong enough for that
long journey and that he had no equipment to fit him
for the task. "I am a Hebrew man. How can I go
amongst the Indians and preach the truth?" During the
night Jesus appeared to Thomas in a vision and said:
"Fear not, Thomas! Go thou into India and preach the
gospel there, for my grace is with thee." But Thomas
was still the stubborn pessimist. "Whither thou wouldst
send me, send me," he said, "but elsewhere, for unto
the Indians I will not go." Now there had come to
Jerusalem from India a merchant called Abbanēs. He
had been sent by King Gundaphorus. (Gundaphorus is
certainly a historical person; coins with his name have
been found.) Abbanēs had been commissioned by
Gundaphorus to find a skilled carpenter, and to bring
him back to India to serve there.

Jesus took on himself the form of a man and came
to Abbanēs in the market place. "Wouldst thou buy a
carpenter?" he asked. Abbanēs answered, "Yes." Jesus
said to him, "I have a slave who is a carpenter, and I
desire to sell him." Jesus pointed out Thomas to Abbanēs. Then and there a deed of sale was drawn up, although Thomas still knew nothing about it, and Thomas was sold to Abbanēs for three litra of silver. Jesus
took Thomas to Abbanēs. Abbanēs said to Thomas,
"Is this thy master?" "Indeed he is," said Thomas. Ab-

banēs said; "I have bought thee from him." And Thomas held his peace. On the next day Thomas rose early and he sought the presence of Jesus. "I will go whither thou will, Lord Jesus," he said. "Thy will be done."

So Thomas went with Abbanēs to India and when they arrived there Abbanēs asked him what he could do. Thomas answered: "In wood I can make ploughs and yokes and oxgoads and boats and oars and masts and pulleys. In stone I can make pillars and temples and courthouses for kings." Abbanēs was glad, for it was just such a craftsman that Gundaphorus needed. So Gundaphorus entrusted Thomas with the task of building a palace for him. They picked a place where there were trees and water. Thomas promised that the palace would be erected with all speed. He took a reed and measured and made his plans. "The doors he set towards the sun rising toward the light, and the windows toward the west to the breezes. The bakehouse he appointed to be toward the south, and the aqueduct for the service toward the north." The king supplied Thomas with abundance of money and provisions, but Thomas did not spend the money in building a palace. He journeyed around the villages and the towns preaching the gospel and distributing the money to the poor and the needy and the afflicted. The king sent word to ask how the building progressed, and Thomas replied that it was completed but for the roof; but nothing had been done to the palace, and all the money had been given away. Thomas prayed to his Master and said, "I thank thee, O Lord, in all things, that thou didst die for a little space that I might live for ever in thee, and that thou has sold me that by me thou mightest set many free." He never ceased to teach and preach and to relieve the afflicted, saying, "This hath the Lord dispensed unto you, and he giveth unto every man his food; for he is the nourisher or orphans and the steward of widows, and unto all that are afflicted he is relief and rest."

The secret could not be kept for ever. It was told to

the king that Thomas had produced no palace at all, but even those who reported Thomas to the king were convinced that Thomas was a saintly man. "He fasteth continually and prayeth, and eateth bread only, with salt, and his drink is water, and he weareth but one garment alike in fair weather and in winter, and receiveth naught of any man, and hath given everything to others."

Finally the king demanded that Thomas should show him the palace. Thomas said, "Thou canst not see it now, but when thou departest this life, then thou shalt see it." The King was enraged, and cast Thomas into prison, and made plans to kill him, and to kill Abbanēs also who had brought him into the country. So Thomas was in prison under sentence of death.

Now Gundaphorus had a brother called Gad and the conduct of Thomas so enraged Gad that his anger made him sick unto death. So angry was he that he died, but, before he died, he made Gundaphorus swear an oath that he would first flay Thomas alive and then burn him in the fire. So Gad died, and when he reached heaven the angels showed him the dwelling places in heaven and asked him where he would like to stay. They came to a great palace, and Gad said that he would delight to live in the humblest room of such a noble place. But the angels told him that palace was already reserved, and that it was not for him. "That is the palace," they said, "which Thomas the Christian builded for thy brother." Then Gad understood. He besought the angels to allow him to return to earth only long enough to tell his brother Gundaphorus what had happened. So he came to earth and asked Gundaphorus to sell him his palace in heaven. Gundaphorus did not know what palace Gad was talking about. Gad explained about the heavenly palace which Thomas had built for him. Then Gundaphorus understood that the money and the goods that Thomas had given to the poor and the afflicted had built for him a palace in the heavenly places. So he summoned Thomas from prison, was baptized by him, and became a devoted Christian.

Such is the legend of Thomas in India, and the legend says that Thomas' body was later brought to Edessa where it lay in the memorial Church which bore his name.

On the whole scholarly opinion holds that the legend of Thomas and India is only a legend, and that the Thomas who had so much to do with the foundation of the India Church was a Nestorian missionary and not the apostle. Robert Sinker in the *Dictionary of Christian Antiquities* sums up the matter: "It would, of course, be rash to claim the legend as authentic history; it is, perhaps, none the less rash to maintain its certain groundlessness; but this latter form of rashness, it would appear, has seemed more justifiable than the former." It is with regret and reluctance that we would have to abandon the legend of Thomas and India; but even if the legend has to go, we may still be certain that the picture it gives of Thomas is true to life and true to character.

No one was ever less of a "stained-glass saint" than Thomas. It was always Thomas' first reaction *not* to do what he was told to do, and *not* to believe what he was asked to believe. The task offered to him was always too hard for him to attempt, and the good news was always too good to be true. But the very fact that Thomas believed with such difficulty made him believe with a fierce intensity once he was convinced. And it was never an argument which solved Thomas' doubts; it was always the presence of his Lord. Thomas again and again made the discovery that every Christian has to make—that by himself everything is impossible, but with God nothing is impossible.

6

MATTHEW

The Man Whom All Men Despised

In one sense we know very little about Matthew, and in another sense we know a great deal about him. We know very little about him personally, but because he was a taxgatherer, we know a great deal about the kind of man he must have been. If we set down side by side the accounts of Matthew's call in the first three Gospels, we shall learn all the known facts about him, and we shall be able to make certain deductions about him.

Mark says: "And as [Jesus] passed by, he saw Levi the son of Alphaeus, sitting at the receipt of custom, and said unto him, Follow me. And he arose and followed him." (2-14.)

Matthew says: "And as Jesus passed forth from thence, he saw a man, named Matthew, sitting at the receipt of custom, and he saith unto him, Follow me. And he rose, and followed him." (9:9.)

Luke says: "And after these things [Jesus] went forth, and saw a publican, named Levi, sitting at the receipt of custom: and he said unto him, Follow me. And he left all, rose up, and followed him." (5:27-28.)

From these passages we learn that Matthew was also called Levi. As we have already seen, it was the regular custom in Palestine for men to have two names. Matthew means the gift of God; and it may be that this also was a name given to Levi by Jesus when he called him, just as he had called Simon by the new name of Peter. We also find that Matthew had most likely a brother in the twelve, for amongst them there was a James, who was also the son of Alphaeus (Matt. 10:3).

The great, outstanding fact about Matthew was that he was a taxgatherer. The K.J.V. calls him a publican. That word has changed its meaning in ordinary English usage. In the Gospels it is derived from the Latin word *publicanus,* which meant a man who was engaged in public service, and especially a man who handled public money, and therefore a taxgatherer.

There was no class of men in the ancient world more hated than taxgatherers. Stapfer calls them "a class of despised pariahs." When Cicero spoke of trades unbecoming to a gentleman and vulgar, he chose as those which incur most odium and ill will, the trades of taxgatherer and usurer (*De Officiis,* 1, 42). In his vision of the underworld Lucian sees a long line of men being led to the throne of Minos where the Tormentors, the Furies, and the Avengers await them; and the long line consists of "adulterers, procurers, tax-collectors, toadies, informers . . . millionaires, and money lenders, pale, pot-bellied, and gouty" (*Menippus,* II).

Of all nations the Jews were the most vigorous haters of taxgatherers. For a strict Jew, God was the only person to whom it was right to pay tribute; to pay tribute to anyone else was to infringe the prerogative which properly belonged to God. "Murderers, robbers, and taxgatherers" were classed together. A taxgatherer was debarred from being either a witness or a judge. He was even debarred from worship, which was why the taxgatherer in the parable stood afar off (Luke 18:13). Even repentance itself was regarded as being specially difficult for a taxgatherer.

It was not only on religious grounds that taxgatherers were hated; they were notoriously rapacious and unjust. When the repentant taxgatherers asked John the Baptist what they must do, his answer was, "Exact no more than that which is appointed you" (Luke 3:13). The Roman method of tax collecting lent itself to abuse. Under the republic the collecting of taxes had been farmed out. Great financial corporations bought the right to collect taxes within a province for a fixed sum. They then proceeded to extract every penny they could from the provincials, and thus they made a handsome profit. Under the republic these taxfarmers often made life a hell for the unfortunate provincials. Under the empire there were great reforms, and the Roman government began either directly to collect the taxes itself, or to exercise a far stricter supervision over those who did. But even under the reformed system government agents were required and abuse was still possible and still prevalent. Strangely enough under the reformed system the taxgatherers themselves were even more bitterly personally hated. Under the old system the great financial corporations to whom the taxes were farmed out had had their own staffs of highly skilled clerks and secretaries and accountants, ready to be sent to any province. But under the new system the government employed as agents people from the provinces themselves, and therefore the taxgatherers were regarded as quislings who had sold themselves into the service of their country's enemies and oppressors for their own private profit.

Broadly speaking there were two kinds of taxes and there were two kinds of tax collectors. There were certain stated taxes. The collector of these was called the *Gabbai,* and in the collecting of these there was little room for extortion and for abuse, because the amount to be paid was known and statutory. These statutory taxes were of three kinds. There was a ground tax, which consisted of one tenth of a man's crop of grain, and one fifth of his produce of wine, fruit, and oil. There was income tax, which was one per cent of a man's income. There was a poll tax, which everyone had to pay simply for the privilege of existing. It was paid by all men between the ages of fourteen and sixty-five, and by all women between the ages of twelve and sixty-five. It probably amounted to one denarius per year. A denarius was a silver coin worth about nine pence, and in evaluating that tax it must be remembered that a man's daily wage in Palestine was normally one denarius per day.

The second kind of tax collector was the *Mokhes*. He was rather like a customs officer. There were great numbers of these customs officers, for government practice was to make one man responsible in one place for the collection of one particular kind of tax or duty, and such taxes and duties were legion. There was an import and an export tax, which was a main source of government revenue. That tax might be anything from two and a half to twelve and a half per cent on the value of the goods imported or exported; or it might be worked on a tariff system on certain articles, as it was in Syria. There was a purchase tax on all that was bought and sold. There was bridge money to be paid when a bridge was crossed; road money to be paid when main roads were used; harbor dues to be paid when a harbor was entered; market money to be paid when a market was used; town dues to be paid when the traveler entered a walled town. If a man was traveling on a road, he might have to pay a tax for using the road, a tax on his cart, on its wheels, on its axle, and on the beast which drew the cart. There was a tax on crossing rivers, on ships, on the use of harbor quays, on dams; there were certain licenses which had to be paid for engaging in certain trades. The Roman peace, the Roman roads, the Roman civil service, the Roman good order and government cost money to run, and the government was fertile in discovering different kinds of taxes to enable it to pay its way.

It was in the collection of these taxes that the customs officer was engaged. He could stop a man anywhere and demand to see his goods. He had the right of search, except in the case of married women. Quintilian (*Declamation,* 359) tells of a Roman matron who could not be searched and who used her immunity to bring in four hundred pearls hidden in the bosom of her dress. The customs officer could at any time compel a man to open his baggage and strip off his clothes, and then he could impose almost any tax that he liked. Tax collectors had been known to compel a traveler to exchange his ass for his own ass, a very inferior beast; tax collectors had been known to assess the duty payable at an impossible sum, and then to offer to lend the sum to the traveler at an impossible rate of interest.

These customs officers were regarded as criminals. It was considered perfectly right to use any subterfuge to. escape their demands. They were ranked with those against whom God had set his face and Lev. 20:5 was said to apply to them. In the New Testament itself they are classed with gentiles (Matt. 18:17), with harlots (Matt. 21:31-33), and with sinners (Matt. 9:10-11; 11:19; Mark 2:15-16; Luke 5:30; 7:34; 15:1).

Such was Matthew. It was in Capernaum that Matthew sat at the receipt of custom (Mark 2:14). For the purposes of government Palestine was divided into two. Samaria and Judea in the south were directly under a Roman procurator, but Galilee in the north was ruled by Herod Antipas, subject to the Romans. Matthew was, therefore, not in the service of the Romans; he was in the service of Herod Antipas. That made little difference to the way in which he was regarded; his opportunities for extortion would be no fewer, and in any event Herod Antipas was a vassal of Rome. The likelihood is that Matthew's was a frontier post. The great road of the east came from Damascus to the Mediterranean seaport of Acre. It first passed through the territory of Ituraea and Trachonitis, which belonged to Philip, Herod's brother, and at Capernaum it entered Galilee and the territory of Herod. It was probably with the traffic on that road and the traffic on the Sea of Galilee itself that Matthew was concerned.

His customs office would be by the seashore, and often he must have listened to Jesus preach and teach. Something in the invitation of Jesus went straight to the heart of Matthew, the outcast and the friendless, and when Jesus called him, Matthew was ready to go. As Luke tells the story, the first thing that Matthew did was to make a feast in his own house for the only friends he had, his fellow tax collectors and other outcasts from society. Matthew's first action when he had found Jesus was to seek to give others the opportunity to meet Jesus. The scribes and the Pharisees were shocked that Jesus should eat with such a company, but Jesus' answer was, "It is not those that are healthy who need a doctor, but those who are sick. Where else should I be?" (See Luke 5:29-31.) Jesus had chosen the man whom all men hated, the man who was supposed to be lost to shame and lost to honor, and had made him one of his men. A more unlikely man to be an apostle it would be impossible to imagine. It took Jesus Christ to see the apostle buried in the tax collector of Capernaum.

Luke in his history of the response of Matthew says that he rose up, left all, and followed Jesus (Luke 5:28). But there was something which Matthew did take with him, and that something was his pen. Ancient tradition is unanimous that Matthew wrote a gospel, and that he wrote it in Hebrew. Eusebius *(The Ecclesiastical History*, 2, 24, 5; cf. Irenaeus, *Against Heresies,* 3, 1; Origen, quoted in Eusebius, 6, 25, 4) says:

Of all the disciples of the Lord only Matthew and John have left us their memoirs; and they, it is reported, had recourse to writing only under the pressure of necessity, for Matthew, who preached earlier to the Hebrews, when he was about to go to others also, committing his gospel in writing in his native tongue, compensated by his writing for the loss of his presence to those from whom he was sent away.

Jerome[1] says,

Matthew who is also called Levi, and who

---

[1] *Concerning Illustrious Men,* 3; cf. *The Prologue to Matthew.*

changed from a tax-gatherer into an apostle, was the
first one in Judaea to write a gospel of Jesus Christ
in Hebrew letters and words for those of the circum-
cision who believed; but who translated it afterwards
into Greek is not sufficiently certain.

The Monarchian Prologues say that Matthew wrote his
Gospel in Judea. Both Eusebius (*The Ecclesiastical
History,* 5, 10, 3) and Jerome (*Concerning Illustrious
Men,* 36) tell us that, when Pantaenus made his expe-
dition to India, he found there a copy of Matthew's
gospel in Hebrew, which Bartholomew was said to
have brought to India. Augustine[2] says that only
Matthew wrote in the Hebrew language and that all the
other gospel writers wrote in Greek. Jerome adds the
information that the Hebrew volume of Matthew's gospel was preserved in the library which Pamphilus had
gathered at Caesarea, although he does not actually
claim to have seen it.

Tradition unanimously ascribes a Hebrew gospel to
Matthew. Modern scholars do not think it likely that
our first gospel is in fact that gospel. Our first gospel is
clearly based on Mark, and it is not likely that Matthew, himself an eyewitness, would have taken over so
much from Mark, and the first gospel certainly does
not read as if it was a translation from the Hebrew.
How then did Matthew's name become attached to the
first gospel?

Papias, the great collector of information about the
Gospels, gives us the clue. Papias says: "Then Matthew
arranged the oracles (*logia*) in the Hebrew dialect, but
everyone interpreted them as he was able." (Quoted in
Eusebius, *The Ecclesiastical History,* 3, 39, 16.) It is
most likely that what Matthew did was to collect and
edit and issue the first collection of the sayings of Jesus.
Now the first Gospel contains more of the teaching of

[2]*Concerning the Agreement of the Gospels,* 1, 2, 4; cf. Cyril of Jerusalem,
Catechesis, 14.

Jesus than any other of the Gospels, as, for instance, in the Sermon on the Mount. So we can believe that Matthew's collection of the sayings, and his account of the teaching of Jesus, formed the basis of the first Gospel, and is incorporated in it, and thus the Gospel came to be called by his name, because his work had contributed so much to it.

Matthew was a tax collector, and, therefore, unlike most of the other apostles, who were fishermen, Matthew could use a pen. When he left his tax collector's table he took his pen with him, and this man, whom once all men despised, became the first man to present to the world an account of the teaching of Jesus. It would clearly be impossible to overestimate the debt we owe to this once despised Matthew.

When we try to trace Matthew outside the Gospels in legend and in tradition, we are in difficulties. The stories differ; the legends are so fantastic that they can have no solid basis in fact; and, to complicate matters, legend and tradition confuse Matthew and Matthias (Acts 1:26). But let us collect the stories, such as they are.

It would appear that Matthew first of all preached the gospel in Judea to his own countrymen, for whom he also wrote his account of the teaching of Jesus (Eusebius, *The Ecclesiastical History,* 3, 24, 5). According to Socrates, when the apostles decided by lot the spheres of their labors, Matthew was allotted Ethiopia (*The Ecclesiastical History,* 1, 19; cf. Rubinus, 1, 9). Ambrose connects him with Persia; Paulinus of Nola with Parthia; Isidore with Macedonia. Even the accounts of his death vary. Clement of Alexandria indicates that he died a natural death (*The Miscellanies,* 4, 9). In passing we may note that Clement passes down the fragment of information that Matthew was a vegetarian, that "he partook of seeds, nuts and vegetables without flesh" (*Paedagogus,* 2, 1). There is a tradition in the Talmud that Matthew was condemned to death

by the Jewish Sanhedrin. There is a late and a legendary account of his martyrdom. The truth is that men
did not clearly know where the work of the gospel took
Matthew in the early days of the faith.

The most famous account of the work of Matthew is
in the Acts of Andrew and Matthew. This account,
fantastic as it is, is doubly famous, for it was put into
Anglo-Saxon verse, perhaps by Cynewulf, the Anglo-
Saxon poet. Matthew, so the story runs, was sent to the
land of the Anthropophagi, the man-eaters, cannibals,
"who ate no bread nor drank wine, but ate the flesh
and drank the blood of men." There Anthropophagi
put out the eyes of strangers, gave them a drug which
took away their senses, and left them thirty days in
prison before finally eating them. So it was done to
Matthew; but the drug was powerless to take his senses
away; and the power of the Lord gave him back his
sight, though his jailers did not know it. Matthew was
held in prison till twenty-seven days of the time of res-
pite was gone.

Word came to Andrew that he must go and rescue
Matthew, and that there were only three days in which
to make the journey. He went with his friends to the
seashore, and found a boat with a steersman and two
others. Andrew did not know it, but the steersman was
Jesus and the two others were angels. They embarked,
and soon there came a terrible storm, but Andrew
calmed the friends who had come with him by telling
them how Jesus had once stilled the storm at sea. Very
wondrously the steersman steered the boat. "Sixteen
years did I sail the sea," said Andrew, "and this is my
seventeenth, and I never saw such steering; the ship is
as if on land." The steersman answered, "Because you
are a disciple of Jesus, the sea knows you and is still."
They had much talk, and finally they came near the
land of the Anthropophagi. Sleep came upon Andrew,
and he awoke to find himself on land, and then he
knew who the steersman of the ship had been. Jesus
came to him again and encouraged him to go on. When

Andrew came to the prison where Matthew was, at his prayer the seven guards fell dead, and at the sign of the Cross the prison doors opened. So Matthew was released together with 270 men and 49 women whom the man-eaters had been keeping for food. Matthew made his escape, but Andrew stayed on. At first he was invisible, and then he showed himself to the people. For days he was terribly ill-treated. They would not behead him, that would have been too easy a death; they dragged him through the city streets, tearing his flesh and spilling his blood, and where his blood touched the ground great fruit trees sprang to life. They put Andrew in prison, and in the prison there was a statue. Andrew touched the statue and from its mouth there came a terrible flood of destroying water which wiped out those whom it touched, and when they tried to flee, they found themselves confronted by a wall of fire. At this the people repented, and Andrew stayed and preached to them for seven days.

The story seems to continue in the Martyrdom of Matthew. Matthew returned to the land of the man-eaters to try to teach them and to civilize them. He cast out devils and he worked many miracles, but the king was jealous of his power. They bound Matthew; covered him with papyrus soaked in dolphin oil; poured brimstone, asphalt, and pitch upon him; heaped up tow and wood; and surrounded him with the golden images of the twelve gods of the people. But the fire turned to dew, and the flames flew out and melted the metal of the images. Finally the fire took the form of a dragon, chased the king into his palace and curled round about him so that he could not move. "Then Matthew rebuked the fire, and prayed, and gave up the ghost." Still more wondrous things happened, and in the end the king was converted and became a priest, and "with two angels Matthew departed to heaven."

These are only legends—fantastic legends—but at the back of them there lies the truth that Matthew preached and died for Jesus Christ. Men would have said that never was there more unpromising material than Matthew, but in the hands of Christ, Matthew became the first man to write down the teaching of Jesus, a missionary of the gospel, and a hero of the faith.

7

JUDAS ISCARIOT

The Man Who Became the Traitor

We may well feel that Judas Iscariot is the supreme enigma of the New Testament, because it is so hard to see how anyone who was so close to Jesus could ever come to betray him into the hands of his enemies.

The name of Judas occurs in the three lists of the twelve apostles (Matt. 10:4; Mark 3:29; Luke 6:16). Matthew and Mark distinguish him by calling him, Judas Iscariot who also betrayed Jesus, and Luke calls him—as it should be translated—Judas Iscariot who became a traitor.

In the first three Gospels Judas does not appear on the scene at all until the drama of the last days, but in the Fourth Gospel he makes two earlier, and significant, appearances.

After the feeding of the five thousand there was a movement to make Jesus king by force (John 6:25). When it became clear that Jesus' aims were very different, many of his supporters drifted away and ceased to follow him. Jesus asked his disciples if they too would leave him. Peter strenuously protested his loyalty; there was none other to whom they could go to find the words of life. It was then that Jesus said, "Have I not chosen you twelve, and one of you is a devil?" John explains that Jesus was referring to Judas Iscariot who was one day to betray him (John 6:66-71).

The Fourth Gospel has its own story of how Mary of Bethany anointed Jesus with the very precious ointment. That was a lovely deed, but the reaction of Judas was that it was a shocking waste, for the ointment could have been sold for three hundred denarii, and the proceeds given to the poor. John's comment is that Judas said this, not because he cared for the poor, but because he had the bag, and, as the K.J.V. has it he bare what was put therein (John 12:1-8). The Greek word which is translated to bear is *bastazein*. Certainly *bastazein* means to bear or to carry; but it also means to pilfer in colloquial Greek. It is like the Scottish use of the verb "to lift." To lift a thing can be to carry it, but may be to steal it, as in the word a shoplifter. What John is saying is that Judas was a covetous man, who used his position as the treasurer of the apostolic band to pilfer from the common purse.

It was in the closing days that Judas played a leading part. The problem of the Jewish authorities was how to get Jesus into their hands without a riot, for Jesus was still popular with the common people. It was Judas who solved their problem for them. "Satan," says Luke, "entered into Judas" (Luke 22:3). He went to the Jewish authorities and undertook for the price of thirty pieces of silver to lead them to a place where they could arrest Jesus without the crowds' being there (Matt. 26:14-16; Mark 14:10,11; Luke 22:3-6). John's timing of the matter seems to be a little different, for as he tells the story, it was at the last meal itself that Satan took possession of Judas, and that Judas formed his purpose of betrayal (John 13:2).

Judas was not allowed to carry out his terrible purpose without a last appeal from Jesus. There are in the Gospels three slightly differing accounts of that appeal. All the Gospels tell how Jesus sorrowfully foretold that one of the twelve would betray him. In Mark and Luke Judas is not mentioned by name, and the warning goes no further (Mark 14:18-21; Luke 22:21-23). In Matthew Judas asks, "Is it I?" and receives the answer, "Thou hast said" (Matt. 26:21-25). John's account (John 13:18-30) is fuller and much more dramatic. To visualize what happened there, we need to try to see how the disciples were placed at that last meal. In the ancient days the guests reclined on low couches, resting

on the left elbow, with the right hand free for the work
of raising the food and the drink. Usually the couches
held three. Clearly John is on Jesus' right, for he was
reclining on Jesus' bosom (John 13:23). But the position in which the most favored guest was placed was on
the host's left, for the host would be reclining with his
head on the breast of the person on his left. When we
read John's narrative, it seems clear that Judas was occupying the place of special honor. At a Passover feast,
amongst other things, there were three things on the
table. There was what was called the *charosheth*, which
was a paste made of apples, dates, pomegranates, and
nuts, and which stood for the clay from which the people had to make bricks in the slavery in Egypt. There
were the bitter herbs, such as endive, horse radish,
chicory, and horehound, which reminded them of the
bitterness of slavery. And there was the unleavened
bread. At one point in the ceremony some of the bitter
herbs were placed between two pieces of unleavened
bread, dipped in the *charosheth*, and eaten. That was
called the sop; and for the host personally to make up
the sop and hand it to a guest was a mark of signal
honor. Jesus handed that sop to Judas (John 13:26),
and the likeliest place for Judas to be sitting was next
to Jesus. Further, the whole atmosphere of the scene is
that Jesus' conversation with Judas was private, that
the other disciples certainly did not know, and hardly
could hear, what was going on between them.

When Judas went out, the others did not know
where he was going. If they had known, he would never
have been permitted to leave that room alive. They
thought that he had gone, because he was treasurer, to
make arrangements for the offering for the poor which
was part of the Passover custom (John 13:29).

So Judas went out—and it was night (John 13:30):
Judas well knew where Jesus would go. So limited was
the space in Jerusalem that there were few or no gardens. Well-to-do people had their private gardens on
the Mount of Olives. Judas knew that some unknown

friend had given Jesus the courtesy of his garden at the
Passover time, and he knew that Jesus would go there.
So Judas led the Jewish authorities there. At the Pas-
over time it was full moon, and the night would be almost as the day. But there was always the chance of
confusion at such a time, and Judas had arranged a
signal whereby he might identify Jesus to the soldiers
and to the Temple police. When a disciple met a
Rabbi, it was the custom for him to place his hands on
his master's shoulders and to kiss him. That was to be
the sign (Matt. 26:47-50; Mark 14:43-45; Luke
22:47). Here there is a possible difference in the accounts. In Luke's account it would be possible to visualize the scene in such a way that Jesus stopped Judas
in the very act, and that the kiss was never given. But
in Matthew and Mark there is something that is very
poignant. The word they use for to kiss is *kataphilein,*
which means to kiss fondly and repeatedly. As we shall
see, that kiss may well have been something much
more than, and very different from, a traitor's kiss.

Then tragedy engulfed Judas. As Matthew tells the
story (Matt. 2:3-10) Judas went back to the priests,
told them that he had sinned against innocent blood,
and besought them to take their money back. When
they would not, he flung it to them and went out and
hanged himself. In this story the end is suicide. A. B.
Bruce says of Judas, "He was bad enough to do the
deed of infamy, and good enough to be unable to bear
the burden of his guilt."

There is a different account in Acts 1:16-20. In
Matthew's account the Jewish authorities used the
money which Judas had flung at them to buy a field for
the burial of strangers, for the money was tainted and
fit for no other use. In the Acts narrative Judas bought
a field with the money, and apparently in the field, met
with a dreadful accident in which his body burst
asunder, and so he died. It is just possible that the Acts
narrative also implies suicide. It says that Judas fell
headlong (Acts 1:18). It could mean either that Judas

hung himself, or that he threw himself down some precipice and so died.

There is still another possible picture of the end of Judas. Moffatt grimly translates Acts 1:18, "Swelling up he burst in two, and all his bowels poured out." The A.S.V. in a footnote indicates that this translation is possibly correct. There is a dreadful early account of the earthly end of Judas quoted in Cramer's *Catena* under Acts 1:18 in a comment cited from Apolinarios, who took the information from Papias. It is there said that Judas contracted some disease whereby he became so swollen with inflammation that a wagon could pass where he could not pass. His head became so swollen that his physician could not even find his eyes. Worms and corruption proceeded from his body, and he suffered the most terrible torments until he died. The place where he died was shunned, because of the intolerable stench which came from it. Another account given by Oecumenius says that Judas was killed by a wagon, and so crushed to death in such a way, that his body burst open. In the early days men piled horror upon horror on the death of the man they regarded as the supreme traitor, the man whom afterwards Dante was to locate in the lowest depth of the ninth circle of hell.

Such, then, are the external facts of Judas' life, but the real problem is the inner working of Judas' mind. It may help to shed light on that question if we can find out what the name Iscariot means.

Jerome suggested that the name Iscariot is connected with the name Issachar, which means gain or reward (Gen. 30:18), and that the reference in the name is to the covetous nature of Judas. T. K. Cheyne suggested that it is connected with the word *hierochitēs,* which means an inhabitant of Jericho, and that thus Judas came from Jericho. It cannot be said that either of these suggestions is likely.

It has been suggested that Iscariot is connected with the word *sikarios,* the Greek form of the Latin *sicarius,* a dagger-bearer. In Acts 21:38 the word *sikarios* is used in the plural to describe the followers of a certain Egyptian revolutionary and in the K.J.V. is translated murderers. In the A.S.V. the word is translated Assassins, the capital letter denoting that the word is not only a description, but is also a title. The *sicarii* were wild and fanatical nationalists, pledged not only to war against the Romans, but to murder and assassination at every opportunity. If this is so, and it is by no means impossible, Judas was a violent Jewish nationalist, who had attached himself to Jesus in the hope that through Jesus his nationalist dreams might be realized. The one fact which makes that meaning unlikely is that Iscariot was certainly the name of Judas' father also. In John 6:71 and 13:26 there is no doubt that the best Greek manuscripts read "Judas Iscariot the son of Simon Iscariot," as indeed the E.R.V., Moffatt, and the A.S.V. translate. Iscariot must mean something which is applicable to father and son alike.

The Syriac versions commonly omit the initial *I* and refer to Judas as Judas Scariot. *Scortya,* in Latin *scoreta,* means a leather coat. John Lightfoot suggested that Judas may have worn such a coat for such coats had pockets which could be used as purses, and Judas was the treasurer of the apostolic band. But if the name Iscariot is to be connected with *scortya* in the case of both Judas and his father, it is much more likely that they were both leatherworkers by trade.

By far the likeliest meaning of Iscariot is that it is a place name. It may well be compounded from *ish,* which is the Hebrew for man, and *Kerioth,* which is a place name. Iscariot would then mean Man of Kerioth. Two Kerioths are mentioned in the Old Testament. One was in Moab (Amos 2:2); the other was in Judea (Joshua 15:25). It is highly unlikely that Judas was a Moabite, because that would mean that he was a gentile, but he may well have come from Judah, and, if he did, he must have been the only non-Galilean in the

apostolic band, a fact which may have been extremely
significant, as we shall see.

Any attempt to paint a picture of Judas as an obvious villain from the beginning is bound to be wrong. It
is curious how little material there is about Judas in
any of the usual apocryphal sources. Almost the only
reference is in The Arabic Gospel of the Infancy.
There is a story there which says that Judas was demon
possessed even when he was a child. The story is that
when both Jesus and Judas were children, they met.
Judas attacked and smote the boy Jesus, whereupon
Jesus cast the devil out of him in the form of a black
dog. But from the narrative of the Gospels we are
bound to conclude that Judas was outwardly exactly
the same as the other disciples. It is clear beyond a
peradventure that, if the other apostles had known
what Judas was about, he would never have been allowed to do it, for they would have acted with swiftness
and with violence, if need be, to protect their Lord.
The very fact that Judas was the treasurer of the twelve
shows that he was trusted. True, John says that he was
a thief (12:6), but it must be remembered that John
was writing seventy years after the events, and was no
doubt seeing meanings which at the time were not seen.

It may well be that it is precisely here that we may
discover one of the reasons why Judas betrayed Jesus.
None of the other apostles saw what was going on in
Judas' heart and mind—but Jesus did. As early as the
events following the feeding of the five thousand Jesus
saw in Judas' heart what W. F. Moulton called "the
germ of the traitor spirit" (John 6:70-71). All the
time the eyes of Jesus were stripping the disguises from
Judas. There may have come a time when Judas could
stand these eyes no longer, and decided that he must
eliminate this Jesus who literally saw through him.

As we have already said, we may receive a clue to
Judas' conduct in the name Iscariot. If Iscariot means
Man of Kerioth Judas was the only non-Galilean in the
apostolic band, the man who was different. Perhaps

from the beginning he had the feeling that he was the
odd man out. There may have been in him a certain
frustrated ambition. It is easy to fail to understand
Judas' position in the twelve. He clearly held a very
important position there. He was treasurer of the
company. Further, Mark describes him in a very re-
markable phrase. In Mark 14:10 the K.J.V. simply
translates the Greek as "Judas Iscariot one of the
twelve." The Greek is a curious phrase, *ho heis tōn
dōdeka,* which literally means the one of the twelve.
Commentators have never been happy about the translation of this phrase, and it is not impossible that what
the Greek means is that Judas was the top one, the
chief one, the one of the twelve. We do not commit
ourselves to that interpretation, but it is certainly a
possibility. Still further, we have already seen that at
the last meal Judas was almost certainly occupying the
place on Jesus' left, the place of highest honor. There
can be no doubt that Judas held a high place among
the twelve—and yet he was not one of the intimate
three—Peter, James, and John. It is not difficult to see
Judas, the one non-Galilean, quite unreasonably de-
veloping the feeling that he was an outsider. It is not
difficult to see him, even if he had a very high place
among the twelve, slowly and unreasonably growing
jealous and embittered because others had a still higher
place. And it is not difficult to see that bitterness coming to obsess him, until in the end his love turned to
hate and he betrayed Jesus.

There is another possibility. It may be that Judas
betrayed Jesus because he saw that the game was up.
This view is capable of two interpretations; (*a*) it may
be that Judas was seeking a cowardly safety, that he
turned king's evidence to save his own skin, when the
inevitable crash came. (*b*) Mark Rutherford thought out
a more subtle variation of this theme. It is clear that
Judas had ideals or he would never have accepted the
call of Jesus. It is clear that he was trusted or he would
never have been made treasurer. It is possible that being

a Judean he was more clear-sighted and coolly able to assess the future than his fellow apostles, who were emotional Galileans. It may, therefore, be that he foresaw a head-on clash with Rome, and that he arranged the arrest of Jesus, not to have Jesus killed, but simply to have him quietly put out of the way and put under restraint before the final damage was done. Mark Rutherford wrote:

> Can any position be imagined more irritating than that of a careful man of business who is keeper of the purse for a company of heedless enthusiasts professing complete indifference to the value of money, misunderstanding the genius of their chief, and looking out every morning for some sign in the clouds, a prophecy of their immediate appointment as viceregents of a power that would supersede the awful majesty of the imperial city?

On this view Judas worked the arrest of Jesus to save him from the catastrophe into which the nationalistic hopes of his followers were driving him.

There is a view of Judas which is the precise opposite of that. If Iscariot is connected with *sikarios,* then Judas was a violent, fanatical nationalist, pledged to use any means to drive the Romans from Palestine. The Jews never ceased to connect their place as the Chosen People with the idea of worldly power and domination. Of all who had that dream the *sicarii* were most fanatical. It may be that Judas saw Jesus, with his powers of speech and action, as the one through whom that dream might be realized. It may have been that it was with that dream that Judas attached himself to Jesus, and he may have seen that dream collapse. It became pitilessly clear that Jesus was driving on, not to world power, but to the cross.

Let us consider two crucial moments in the life of Judas. One came immediately after the people wished to take Jesus and to make him king (John 6:15). It was then that Jesus saw in him the traitor (John 6:70-71). It was then, as it has been put, that "there crystallized in the heart of Judas the evil and diabolic purpose which made him an adversary of the man whom he had called friend." In that moment Judas saw the death of his dream, and he hated this Jesus who had killed the dream.

Let us think of the second great moment in what has been called "the demonizing of Judas." When did it happen? (Matt. 26:14-16; Mark 14:10-11; Luke 22:3-6). It happened immediately after the Triumphal Entry. The Triumphal Entry might have been the moment when Jesus raised the standard of revolt and stormed as warrior king into Jerusalem. Instead of that it was the moment when Jesus began the last mile to the cross. Again Judas saw his dream being crucified. This time he took action. His love had turned to hate, and he took vengeance for the death of his dream by betraying the man who had killed it into the hands of his enemies. If this be so, Judas betrayed Jesus because love had turned to hate, because Jesus refused to be what he wanted him to be.

We cannot altogether omit from the motives of Judas the motive which is most obvious of all, the element of greed for money and love of gain. If that is so, Judas struck one of the most dreadful bargains in history when he betrayed Jesus for thirty pieces of silver, about fourteen dollars, the normal value of a slave (Exod. 21:32). It may just possibly be that by this time Jesus had a price upon his head, and that Judas betrayed him to gain that price (cf. John 11:57).

There is somehow a certain inadequacy about any of the motives which we have so far produced. Maybe the real motive was this. Judas was the violent nationalist, the man with the dream. He had not the slightest doubt that Jesus could make that dream come true. He saw that Jesus was strangely and inexplicably slow to act, and he decided, as De Quincey suggested, to force Jesus' hand, and to compel him to act. If that is so, the last thing in Judas' mind was any desire that Jesus should be crucified; the only thing in his mind was to create a situation in which Jesus would be compelled to unleash his power. If that is so, there is real drama in the scene in the garden. When Judas kissed Jesus, maybe there was a blaze of excitement on his face and a flame of expectation in his eyes. "Hail, master!" he said (Matt. 26:49). On to victory! Unleash your power!

There are real reasons for thinking that herein lay the motive of Judas. Why is it that after that moment in the garden Judas vanishes from the scene? Why is it that he did not appear in court to give evidence against Jesus? What more effective evidence could there have been than evidence from one of Jesus' closest supporters? Why did he commit suicide? The reason may well be that in one searing moment Jesus saw how tragically far wrong his carefully thought-out plan had gone, and that he had killed the man he loved. Judas was the man whose tragedy was that he refused to accept Jesus Christ as he was, and sought to make Jesus Christ into what he wanted him to be.

All through Christian history men have sought to see into the mind of Judas. We cannot and dare not say that Jesus chose Judas in order that he might betray him, nor can we say that Jesus chose Judas knowing that he would betray him. Such an idea would be little short of blasphemy, for it would mean nothing less than that Jesus deliberately placed a man in a position where deadly sin was inevitable. In his magnificent article on Judas in *The Dictionary of Christ and the Gospels*, J. G. Tasked quotes two verdicts on Judas. Lavater said of Judas, "Judas acted like Satan, but like a Satan who had it in him to be an apostle." Pressensé said of Judas, "No man could be more akin to a devil than a perverted apostle." And in these sayings the potential greatness and the actual fall of Judas are summed up.

The New Testament rings down the curtain on Judas in Acts 1:25 where it was said that Matthias was cho-

sen to take part in the ministry and the apostleship
from which Judas had fallen "that he might go to his
own place." What Judas' own place was is not for us to
say. But one of the loveliest things that was ever said
by any preacher or commentator was said by Origen
about Judas. Origen suggested that, when Judas realized what he had done, he rushed to commit suicide in
order that he might meet Jesus in Hades, the world of
the dead, and there with bared soul implore his Lord's
forgiveness (*Sermons on Matthew*, 35). Mark Rutherford ends his essay on Judas by saying that no witnesses were ever called on Judas' behalf, and Judas
never told his own story:

> What would his friends of Kerioth have said for
> him? What would Jesus have said? If he had met
> Judas with the halter in his hand, would he not have
> stopped him? Ah! I can see the divine touch on the
> shoulder, the passionate prostration of the repentant
> in the dust, the hands gently lifting him, the forgive-
> ness for he knew not what he did, and the seal of a
> kiss indeed from the sacred lips.

When we feel ourselves mercilessly condemning
Judas Iscariot because he betrayed his Lord, let us remember that Jesus once said, "He that is without sin
among you, let him first cast a stone" (John 8:7).

8

JAMES, THE BROTHER OF JESUS

The Enemy Who Became the Friend

James, the brother of Jesus, was not one of the original twelve. He, indeed, began by being an opponent of Jesus. But the day was to come when James was to be the leader of the Jewish side of the Christian Church, the president of the church in Jerusalem, as he has been called, and a martyr for the faith.

Our justification for calling James an apostle comes from the way in which Paul speaks about him. When Paul was describing his first visit to Jerusalem as a converted man, he tells of his meeting with Peter, and then he says, "But other of the apostles saw I none, save James the Lord's brother" (Gal. 1:19). It is true that there are some New Testament scholars who deny that that sentence implies that James was an apostle, and who insist that it means, "I saw Peter, and no other of the apostles—but only James." But we are certain that the plain meaning of the words is that to Paul and to the Christian Church James ranked as an apostle, and certainly James was the undisputed leader of the Jerusalem church.

There is much that we do not know about James, and there is much that we can only guess, but this much is certain—James was a man whose attitude toward Jesus underwent a revolutionary change. At the beginning of his ministry we find Jesus and his family on the move together. We find them at Cana (John 2:1), and at Capernaum (John 2:12). But it is clear that there came an ever-widening breach. They came to regard Jesus as mad (Mark 3:21), or as one to be restrained from his folly, and to be brought home again

(Mark 3:31-33). We find them trying to taunt him
into action, because, as John says, "neither did his
brethren believe in him" (John 7:5). We listen to
Jesus poignantly saying, "A man's foes shall be they of
his own household" (Matt. 10:36), and these were the
words of personal experience.

Then there comes a change, and a change which in
the New Testament record seems at first sight to be
unexplained. When Luke is listing the people gathered
together after the Cross, the Resurrection, and the
Ascension, he includes the brothers of Jesus (Acts
1:14). As we go further on we find that James has
emerged as the supreme leader of the Jerusalem
church. When Peter was released from prison, his first
act was to send word to James and to the brethren
(Acts 12:17). When the all-important question of the
reception of the gentiles into the Church arose, it was a
clear-speaking, clear-thinking speech by James in his
capacity as leader of the Church which settled the issue
(Acts 15:13-21). When Paul came to Jerusalem with
the collection for the poor, it was by James and the
elders that he was received (Acts 21:18). When we
turn to Paul's letters, it is the same. On his first visit to
Jerusalem after his conversion, it was James and Peter
whom he met (Gal. 1:19). On his visit fourteen years
later, James, Peter, and John are the pillars of the
Church, and it is they who affirm the agreement that
Paul must be the apostle to the gentiles (Gal. 2:9). It
is a long way from James the enemy of Jesus to James
the leader of the Jerusalem church.

When we leave the New Testament and proceed further into the history of the early Church, we find that
James died a martyr for Jesus Christ. We have two accounts of his death. One comes to us in the writings of
Josephus the Jewish historian. During the brief inter-
regnum which occurred between the death of Festus,
the Roman governor, and the arrival of Albinus the
next governor, Ananus, the high priest, seized the opportunity to do as he liked.

So Ananus, being that kind of man, and thinking that he had got a good opportunity, because Festus was dead and Albinus not yet arrived, held a judicial council; and he brought before it the brother of Jesus, who was called Christ—James was his name —and some others, and on the charge of violating the Law he gave them over to be stoned. (*Antiquities of the Jews,* 20, 9, 1.)

Hegesippus the Christian historian gives us a much longer and fuller account of the death of James, which is passed down to us by Eusebius. (*The Ecclesiastical History,* 2, 23.) That account runs as follows. James lived a life of such holiness and piety that he was respected by all. He had never ceased rigorously and meticulously to keep the Jewish Law, and Christians and Jews alike regarded him as a saint. "He was holy from his mother's womb; wine and strong drink he drank not, nor did he eat flesh; no razor touched his head; he never anointed himself with oil; and he used not the bath." His knees were as hard as a camel's because he was so constant in prayer and in entreaty to God for pardon for the people. Because of his piety he was called The Just, and Oblias, which means The Bulwark of the People.

From the story it becomes clear that the Jewish authorities did not realize where James stood in his belief. They must have been misled by his careful keeping of the Law. They were alarmed at the number of people who were becoming Christians, and they came to James and said: "We entreat you to restrain the people who are led astray after Jesus . . . for we all have confidence in you. Persuade them not to be led astray. Stand, therefore, on the wing of the Temple that your words may be heard by all the people." It was Passover time and the city was crowded. So they placed James on the wing of the Temple, but his message was not what they expected or desired to hear. "Why do you

ask me concerning Jesus the Son of Man?" he cried.
"He is now sitting in the heavens on the right hand of
the Great Power, and he is about to come on the
clouds of heaven." The Jewish leaders were enraged.
"We were wrong," they said, "to permit such a testi-
mony to Jesus; let us go up and cast him down that
through fear the people may not believe in him." "Ho!
Ho!" they said, "even the Just has gone astray."

So they hurled him down from the Temple pinnacle,
and stoned him; and as they stoned him he prayed, "I
beseech thee, God and Father, forgive them, for they
know not what they do." One of the priests tried to
stop the murder. "Stop your stoning," he cried, "the
Just One is praying for you." But a fuller ran up and
beat out James's brains with the club he used to beat
his clothes. And so James died. Scholars may question
the details of the narrative of the death of James; the
fact remains that James died for the name of the
brother whom he had once held in contempt.

Wherein lies the explanation? How did James the
enemy become James the martyr?

Within the New Testament itself the explanation is
given. When Paul was recounting the appearance of the
risen Lord, he gives his list of these appearances, and
then he says, "After that, he was seen of James" (I
Cor. 15:7). Jesus made a special resurrection appearance to James. The New Testament has no details of
that appearance, but the story is amplified in the Gospel according to the Hebrews, a very early gospel
which failed to gain a place in the New Testament.
Most of it is lost, but the passage which tells of the appearance of Jesus to James was preserved by Jerome in
his brief biography of James (*Concerning Illustrious
Men*, 2):

> Now the Lord, when he had given the linen cloth
> unto the servant of the High Priest, went unto James
> and appeared to him (for James had sworn that he
> would not eat bread from that hour wherein he had

drunk the Lord's cup, until he should see him risen
again from among them that sleep). And again after
a little, "Bring ye," saith the Lord, "a table and
bread." And immediately, it is added, he took bread
and blessed and break it, and gave it unto James the
Just, and said unto him, "My brother, eat thy bread,
for the Son of Man is risen from among them that
sleep."

That passage is not without its problems. It implies that
James was present at the Last Supper. The beginning
of it seems to say that when Jesus arose from the dead,
he handed the linen shroud in which he had been
wrapped in death to the servant of the high priest, who
must have been on guard at the tomb. But the one fact
is certain—that Jesus appeared to James. Something in
the last days may well have caught at James's heart;
something in the last meal and in the Cross may well
have shown him how tragically wrong he had been in
his assessment of his brother; and he had taken a vow
that he would starve until Jesus came back to him. It
was the sacrificial love of the Cross and the power and
the presence of the Resurrection which changed James
the enemy into James who was faithful unto death. A
Christian is always a man whose heart has been broken
by the Cross, and whose life has been renewed by the
Resurrection.

9

PHILIP

The First Man Called to Follow Jesus

Philip is another of the apostles who has been rescued from oblivion by the Fourth Gospel. The first three Gospels record nothing about him except his name (Matt. 10:3; Mark 3:18; Luke 6:14; Acts 1:13). In the Fourth Gospel Philip becomes a person and a personality.

Before we begin to put together the facts about Philip, we must enter a caution. Philip the apostle is always liable to be confused with the Philip who was one of the seven (Acts 6:5). In point of fact we know more about Philip of the seven than we know about Philip the apostle. It was the Philip of the seven who had the astonishingly successful campaign in Samaria (Acts 8:5-14), and was the means of the conversion of the Ethiopian eunuch (Acts 8:26-40); and it was also this Philip with whom Paul stayed in Caeserea (Acts 21:8). The Philip who was one of the seven was a major figure in the missionary enterprise of the early Church.

Even the most reliable authorities in the early Church confused the two Philips. Tertullian speaks of the apostle Philip being snatched away from the Ethiopian eunuch (*Concerning Baptism,* 18). Even so reputable a historian as Eusebius refers Acts 21:8 to the apostle Philip (*The Ecclesiastical History,* 3, 31, 5). In the calendar of the Coptic and the Armenian Churches there is a commemoration of Philip as "deacon and apostle." Even in the early days, men found it very difficult to remember that there were two Philips, and to differentiate between them.

It is of interest to note that Eric F. F. Bishop in his book *Apostles of Palestine* thinks it not impossible that the Philip of Acts 8 is indeed the apostle, and that Tertullian may be right in saying so. That chapter begins by saying that because of the intensity of the persecution in Jerusalem, the Christians were scattered abroad, with the exception of the apostles. Verse 5 goes on to say that Philip went down to Samaria. The verb used is *katerchesthai,* which is the regular word for a journey from Jerusalem to Samaria and would describe the journey Philip made if he went from Jerusalem to Samaria. The thing which almost definitely precludes this theory is that after the successful preaching of this Philip in Samaria, Peter and John went down from Jerusalem to Samaria in order that through the hands of an apostle the Samaritans might receive the Holy Spirit (Acts 8:14). Had this Philip been an apostle, the visit of other apostles would not have been necessary. But let us come to our definite information about Philip.

Philip came from Bethsaida, the town from which Peter and Andrew came (John 1:44), and, if Philip came from Bethsaida, the likelihood is that he too was a fisherman.

As John tells the story, Philip was the first man to whom Jesus addressed the words, "Follow me!" (John 1:43). Even if Philip never emerged from the background to the foreground, and even if he remains a man about whom we know very little, he has the imperishable distinction of being the first man to hear the Master's "Follow me!" Thereafter Philip makes four appearances in the Fourth Gospel, and each appearance adds to our knowledge of him.

1. After his call by Jesus, Philip's first action was to find Nathanael and to tell him of this Jesus whom he had discovered and who had discovered him. He told Nathanael that they had found him of whom Moses and the prophets spoke. But Nathanael was skeptical. "Can there any good thing come out of Nazareth?" he

asked. Philip did not argue; he answered, "Come and see" (John 1:45-46).

This incident tells us two things about Philip. First, he had the missionary instinct. The moment he had found Jesus Christ for himself, he was determined to share Christ with others. Discovery and communication go hand in hand. Second, Philip had the right approach to the skeptic. He did not argue; he may have been well aware that Nathanael could have sunk him in any battle of argument. He simply said, "Come and see!" Argument often only obscures; confrontation sweeps away a man's defences.

2. The next time we meet Philip is at the feeding of the five thousand. It is to Philip that Jesus addresses the question, "Whence shall we buy bread, that these may eat?" And Philip answers, "Two hundred pennyworth of bread is not sufficient for them that every one of them may take a little (John 6:5-7).

Two interesting suggestions have been made about this scene. It has been suggested that Philip was in charge of the commissariat of the twelve, and that, when it was a matter of feeding arrangements, Jesus naturally turned to him. It has also been suggested that the answer of Philip comes so immediately and so unhesitatingly that he must already have been calculating in his own mind how this multitude could be fed. Milligan in his article on Philip in *The Dictionary of Christ and the Gospels* points out that in Palestine one denarius normally bought twelve wheaten or thirty-six barley "loaves" a span in diameter and about an inch and a half thick. Maybe Philip was calculating the irreducible minimum necessary to give every person in the crowd a bite! A denarius was a working man's pay for a day. It is as if Philip said, "A year's pay would not buy enough to give this crowd a bite apiece!"

From this incident we may see that Philip was a man with a warm heart and pessimistic head; he was one of those many people who would very much like to do something for others, but who do not see how it can possibly be done. Cavour said that the supreme essential of a statesman was "a sense of the possible." Philip —and he has many descendants—had a vivid sense of the impossible, for he had yet to learn that little is much in the hands of Christ, and that with God all things are possible.

3. The next time we meet Philip is in the last days of Jesus' life. Certain Greeks had come to Jerusalem, and they came to Philip with a request to see Jesus. They probably came to Philip because Philip is a typically Greek name, and because they thought that their best chance of establishing contact with Jesus was through a man with such a name. Philip's reaction was to go to Andrew and to tell him; and only then did Andrew and Philip bring the Greeks to Jesus (John 12:20-22).

Here we see Philip as the man who disliked responsibility, and who recoiled from having important decisions thrust upon him. When a man is like that in temperament, he can adopt either of two courses. He can simply let the matter slide, and by so doing can come to a decision by evading any decision at all. Or, he can refer the matter to someone whom he knows to have a stronger and more decisive character than his own. The second way is the way of self-knowledge and of wisdom. That was what Philip did, and that is the proof that Philip knew his own weakness and that he was a wise man.

4. The last time we meet Philip is in the Upper Room. Jesus was talking about the Father and how he was going to the Father. Philip was a man for whom faith was difficult. "Lord," he said, "shew us the Father, and it sufficeth us." Philip received what is maybe the greatest answer Jesus ever gave any one: "He that hath seen me hath seen the Father" (John 14:8-9). For Philip, to believe involved to see. But Philip did not bottle up and restrain his questioning mind. He took his question to Jesus; and Philip that night learned that if we want to see what God is like we must look at

Jesus—and that is the central truth of the Christian religion. A. E. Baker says that for William Temple "the central fundamental affirmation of the Christian religion is that Jesus of Nazareth is the unique, final manifestation of God." That is what Philip discovered, because he was not afraid or ashamed to take his problem to Jesus.

When we leave the New Testament we find many legends about Philip, but they are fantastic works of fiction. Before we mention any of them, we note one very odd report about Philip. Clement of Alexandria (*The Miscellanies*, 3. 4) relates, as if it were an accepted fact, that Philip was the man who wished to follow Jesus, but who desired first of all to go and bury his father (Luke 9:59). How that legend arose it is difficult to see, for Philip had come to his decision long before that.

As we have said the apocryphal Acts of Philip are a tissue of wild impossibilities. We take one section (section 2) as a sample. Philip, so the story runs, went to Athens. Three hundred philosophers gathered to hear him, for the Athenians ever sought to hear something new. Peter preached about Jesus. The philosophers asked for three days to think it over. They came to the conclusion that the best way would be to send to the Jewish high priest at Jerusalem to get, as they thought, a clear and informed account of the matter. Ananias, the high priest, came to Athens with five hundred men to destroy Philip. Philip smote them all with blindness. Philip ordered the earth to swallow Ananias to the knees, but Ananias declared that this was witchcraft. Then Philip ordered the earth to swallow him to the waist, but still Ananias was obdurate; then to the neck, but still Ananias would not yield. Finally after many other miracles, Philip ordered the earth to swallow Ananias, which it did, and as he was swallowed up, his high-priestly robe flew away, and to this day no one knows where it is! The five hundred Jews who had come with Ananias were converted and baptized together with many of the Athenians, and Philip stayed two years in Athens, and founded a church there.

Legend takes him to many places—to Lydia, to Asia, to Parthia, and to Gaul—but legend is fairly unanimous that Philip became one of the great lights of Asia (Eusebius, *The Ecclesiastical History*, 3, 21), and that he was martyred at Hierapolis.

The legend of his martyrdom exists. He came to Hierapolis and found the people worshipping a great snake. With him were Bartholomew and Mariamne. Philip preached with great success, which aroused the hatred and enmity of the proconsul. Philip was stripped, pierced in the ankles and thighs and hung head downwards. Then follows a curious episode. Philip refused to tolerate such treatment, although the others, including John, who by this time had appeared on the scene, urged him not to render evil for evil. He ordered the ground to open up and swallow the people, and seven thousand people were swallowed up. Then Jesus himself appeared and rebuked Philip for his anger and restored to life the people whom Philip's action had destroyed. Then Philip, still hanging head downwards, confessed his fault, and suffered until he died. As he died he made a strange request. He asked that his dead body should be wrapped, not in linen, but in papyrus, for he was not worthy that even his dead body should be treated as the body of Jesus had been treated. "And they buried him as he had directed. And a heavenly voice said that he had received his crown."

So Philip in the end was faithful unto death.

10

SIMON THE ZEALOT

*The Man Who Began by Hating
and Ended in Loving*

Simon the Zealot is a man about whom we know so
little that even his name produces problems. The New
Testament tells us nothing but his name, and in the
K.J.V. the designation by which he is called differs
from place to place. In Matthew and Mark he is Simon
the Canaanite (Matt. 10:4; Mark 3:18); in two other
places he is Simon who is called Zēlōtēs (Luke 6:15;
Acts 1:13). In Moffatt he is called Simon the Zealot in
all four places. In the E.R.V. and the A.S.V. he is
called Simon the Cananaean in Matthew and Mark,
and Simon the Zealot in Luke. In the Luke passages
there is no difficulty, for Simon is called by the Greek
word *zēlōtēs,* which means a zealot. The problem lies
in the Matthew and Mark passages. There the Greek
manuscripts have two readings. The inferior manuscripts, which the K.J.V. followed, read *Kananitēs,*
which the K.J.V. translates Canaanite. That is quite certainly wrong. The Greek for Canaan is *Chanaan,* and the
adjective from it is *Chananaios.* If *Kananitēs* is to be accepted at all, then it must be translated Cananite, not
Canaanite, as indeed the earlier English versions, such
as the Geneva Bible, did transliterate it. Jerome in his
Commentary on Matthew did accept the reading *Kananitēs,* but connected it with Cana in Galilee. There-
from arose the conjecture that Simon was none other
than the bridegroom of the marriage feast in Cana in
Galilee, and the story that after the feast he became a
disciple and a follower of Jesus. This interpretation we
have regretfully to abandon, because the adjective from

Cana is *Kanaios,* not *Kananitēs.* The reading of the best
and most ancient manuscript is *Kananaios,* which is the
word which the E.R.V. and the A.S.V. transliterate cor-
rectly Cananaean. This word is derived from the Hebrew
verb *kana,* which means to be jealous; and it was used
for those who were jealous for the Law; *zēlōtēs* is precisely the same word in Greek; it also means one who
is jealous. And in this case the jealousy is of those who
were jealous for the sanctity and the honor of the Law.
Cananaean is the correct reading, and *Cananaean* and
Zealot are the same word, the first in Hebrew, the second in Greek.

It is this which gives us our key to Simon. We know
nothing about him personally, but if he was a Zealot,
we know very well what kind of beliefs he once held
and what kind of man he once was for we have ample
evidence to form a picture of the Zealots and their
characteristic beliefs.

The Zealots were the last of the great Jewish parties
to emerge, and although according to their lights, they
were the most fervent patriots of all, they were nonetheless directly responsible for the final destruction of
the Jewish state.

Palestine was a subject country under the Roman
rule and the Jews had never learned to accept the fact.
Even in days when the Jews were well governed and
when there were peace and prosperity, Palestine was
always at best a sleeping volcano, ready and liable to
erupt into violence. For many years Herod the Great
had succeeded in holding the nation together in some
kind of peace. He did it by sheer force of personality,
and by his skill in diplomacy, which enabled him to
work with the Romans and to extract privileges for the
Jews from them. He died in 4 B.C. He divided up his
territory between his sons. To Philip he left the regions
of Ituraea and Trachonitis in the northeast; to Herod
Antipas he left Galilee; and to Archelaus he left Judea
and Samaria. This arrangement had to be ratified by
the Roman overlords, of course, and before it could be

ratified, Palestine erupted. The blaze was fiercest in
Galilee. There Judas the Galilean raised an insurrection, stormed the palace of Sepphoris, broke into the
arsenal, armed his followers, and embarked on a revolution. In course of time the Roman power speedily
broke Judas but it was directly from him that the
Zealots stemmed.

The Romans did ratify Herod's disposition of his
territory, but Archelaus proved unfit to rule, and the
Romans were compelled to introduce a Roman governor into Judea. The governor was Quirinius (cp. Luke
2:2, where he is called Cyrenius). Quirinius took the
normal Roman step of instituting a census for the purposes of taxation and administration, and promptly the
country exploded in revolution. For the rigid Jew God
was the only king, and God was the only person to
whom tribute could be paid. This revolt was not a political insurrection, but a holy war. Once again Judas
was at the head, but this time the revolt was mercilessly
crushed, and Judas was killed. Out of this bloodshed
the Zealots arose.

Years before this the Jews had been confronted with
the savage attempt of Antiochus Epiphanes to obliterate their nation and their faith. In those days the Maccabees had arisen to be the saviours of their country;
and when Mattathias, the father of the Maccabees, was
dying, his parting message was: "And now, my children, be zealous for the Law, and give your lives for
the covenant of your fathers" (I Macc. 2:50). So the
Zealots were fanatical Jewish patriots who were zealous
for the Law and bitter haters of the foreign power. Josephus more than once describes them.

Judas the Galilaean was the author of the fourth
act of Jewish philosophy. . . . They [the Zealots]
have an inviolable attachment to liberty, and say that
God is their only Ruler and Lord. They do not mind
dying any kind of death, nor do they heed the tor-
ture of their kindred and their friends, nor can any

such fear make them call any man lord. And since this immovable resolution of theirs is known to a great many, I shall speak no further about that matter; for I am not afraid that anything that I have said about them will be disbelieved, but rather fear that what I have said comes short of the resolution they show when they undergo pain *(The Antiquities of the Jews, 18, 1, 6)*.

So, then, the Zealots were fanatical Jewish nationalists who had a heroic disregard for the sufferings involved in the struggle for what they regarded as the purity of their faith.

Any such party runs a danger. Such fanaticism can come very near to madness. And any such party can, and will, attract to itself adventurers and men of violence who will use the general situation for their own ends. The Zealots developed into the *sicarii,* the Assassins. The Assassins were sworn to a career of murder and assassination. They received their name from the *sica,* the little curved sword, which they carried below their robes, and which they plunged into the bodies of their enemies at every possible opportunity. The Assassins were not so much patriots as they were terrorists.

Two things happened as Palestine began to break up. The Zealots and the Assassins at their lowest used the opportunities of guerilla warfare to burn and plunder villages and towns, partly in a sheer passion of destruction, partly as acts of brigandage. Still further, they began to turn their weapons and their violence, not only against the Romans, but even against their own countrymen. If they thought that any Jew was willing to compromise or to enter into any treaty or agreement with the Romans, such a Jew was marked for assassination. One of the most terrible times in history was the last siege of Jerusalem in A.D. 70. The Romans, weary of the troubles of Palestine, had determined to settle things once and for all. When Jerusalem

was besieged, when the inhabitants were slowly starv-
ing to death, and when the outlook was completely
hopeless, within the besieged city a civil war was raging
and the Zealots and the Assassins were murdering anyone who suggested a more moderate policy, or who was
prepared to come to terms before ultimate ruin
engulfed the city. The Zealots and the Assassins were
crazed with hatred for the Romans and for anyone who
had anything to do with the Romans. It was their in-
sane hatred of Rome which in the end destroyed their
city.

Josephus says of them, "Zealots, for that was the
name those reckless persons went by, as if they were
Zealous in good practices, and were not rather extrava-
gant and reckless in the worst actions." (*Wars of the
Jews,* 4, 3, 9.)

Nothing shows the fanaticism of the Zealots better
than the incident in which the last of them finally
perished. When Jerusalem fell, some strongholds did
not surrender. The last of them was Masada, where a
group commanded by Eleazar still held out. When it
was clear that all hope of escape was gone, Eleazar
summoned them and made a flaming speech in which
he urged them first to slaughter their own wives and
children, and then to commit suicide. They took him at
his word. "They tenderly embraced their wives, kissed
their children, and then began the bloody work. Nine
hundred and sixty perished; only two women and five
children escaped by hiding in a cave." (*Wars of the
Jews,* 7, 8, 9.)

That is the background of Simon the Zealot. Simon
was a man who was a fanatical nationalist, a man devoted to the Law, a man with bitter hatred of anyone
who dared to compromise with Rome. Since that is so,
two things emerge.

1. The constitution of the twelve presents us with a
situation which is nothing less than a miracle in personal relationships. Within that society there was
Matthew the tax collector and Simon the Zealot—

Matthew who had accepted the political situation, and who was profitably engaged in help to administer it, and Simon who would have assassinated any Roman whom he could reach and would have plunged a dagger into any Jew who dared to co-operate with the Romans. The plain truth is that, if Simon had met Matthew under any other circumstances, he would have murdered him. Matthew was the very kind of person who topped the list of candidates for the Assassin's dagger. Here is one of the greatest of all examples of personal enmity destroyed by common love of Christ. If Matthew and Simon could live at peace within the apostolic band, then there is no breach between men which cannot be healed when men love Christ.

2. After the Cross Simon was still there (Acts 1:13). Here is the proof that Simon had come to see that the dagger must abdicate for the Cross. Simon had dedicated his life to reformation by power politics, and he had come to accept the way of sacrificial love.

We may briefly follow Simon into legend. Even legend is vague about him. He is said to have preached in Egypt, in Africa, and even in Britain. The only extended notice of him is in *The Apostolic History* of Abdias (6, 7-21). The story there runs as follows. Simon with Jude found his way to Persia. The opposition to them and to their preaching was led by two magicians called Zaroës and Arfaxat. At every turn Zaroës and Arfaxat were defeated by the power and the wisdom of Simon and Jude. In particular they were defeated in the giving of advice to the king, and in a contest of magical power. "Kill them outright," said the king. But the apostles refused. "Our God does not ask for forced service," they said. "If you will not believe, you may go free."

So Zaroës and Arfaxat were freed, but so far from being either convinced or grateful, they pursued a campaign of slander against Simon and Jude up and down the country. Wherever Simon and Jude went they preceded them, warning and inciting the people against

them. Simon and Jude came to the city of Suanir,
where there were seventy priests and a great temple.
The people were roused against them. "Bring out the
enemies of our gods," they shouted. So Simon and Jude
were brought into the temple and given the alternative
of sacrifice or death. Jude said to Simon, "I see the
Lord calling us." Simon answered, "I see him also
among the angels; moreover an angel has said to me:
Go out hence and the temple shall fall. But I said: No,
for some here may be converted." The angel then gave
them a choice. Either they could escape and all the
people and the temple could be destroyed, or they
could suffer martyrdom. "Choose either the death of all
here or the palm of martyrdom." They chose the
palm, for Simon and Jude would not save their lives by
destroying the lives of others. The priests and the people attacked them and slew them, and so they died.

Whatever be the truth in that story, even if it be
nothing more than pious fiction, it is symbolically true.
Simon, the man who once would have murdered people
into loyalty, became the man who saw that God will
have no forced service. Simon, the man who once
would not have scrupled to obliterate his enemies, was
the man who would not buy his life at the price of the
lives of others.

11

JAMES, THE BROTHER OF JOHN

*The Man Who Was the First
of the Twelve to Become a Martyr*

James, the brother of John and the son of Zebedee, is the most tantalizingly vague figure among the twelve. That he occupied a leading place among the apostles is beyond doubt. He was the first of them to gain the martyr's crown (Acts 12:2). In every list of the apostles he is in the first three. In the lists of Mark and Acts his name comes second only to that of Peter (Mark 3:17; Acts 1:13); and in the lists of Matthew and Luke it comes third after the names of Peter and Andrew (Matt. 10:2; Luke 6:14). It may be that his name comes before that of John, because he was the elder of the two brothers. Yet although James occupied so prominent a place among the twelve, we know almost nothing about him.

The difficulty in reconstructing a picture of James is that he never at any time in his life appears apart from John. John and James in the gospel story constitute an inseparable pair. Let us, then, briefly recapitulate the facts about James and John.

They were fishermen, and they were the sons of Zebedee, who was sufficiently well-to-do to be able to employ hired servants in his business (Mark 1:19-20). They were called by Jesus to become fishers of men, and they accepted the challenge and the invitation (Matt. 4:19; Mark 1:20; cf. Luke 5:1-11). In the apostolic band James and John constituted, along with Peter, an inner circle who were with Jesus on the most sacred occasions (cf. pp. 18, 28). They were typically impulsive and quick-tempered Galileans, and their vi-

olence of temper earned for them the name of sons of
thunder, Boanerges (Mark 3:17). It was this explosive
temper which made them wish to blot out the Samaritan village which refused hospitality to Jesus and the
rest of their company (Luke 9:51-56). They were
ambitious men who desired for themselves the leading
places in the coming kingdom of Christ (Mark 10:35-
45; Matt. 20:20-28).

James's one appearance by himself is his martyrdom,
which the New Testament story tells in two brief
verses: "Now about that time Herod the king stretched
forth his hand to vex certain of the church. And he
killed James the brother of John with the sword. (Acts
12:1-2.)

Such is the sum total of our knowledge of James.
But there are certain legends about him. Eusebius relates a story about James which he found in the seventh
book of the lost *Hypotyposes* of Clement of Alexandria. Eusebius writes:

> He says that the one who led James to the judg-
> ment seat, when he saw him bearing his testimony,
> was moved and confessed that he also was a Chris-
> tian. They were both, therefore, Clement says, led
> away together; and on the way he begged James to
> forgive him. And he, after considering a little, said:
> Peace be with thee, and kissed him. And thus they
> were both beheaded at the same time.

So James was one of that noble army of martyrs whose
constancy converted even their accusers.

The Apostolic History of Abdias connects James
with two magicians called Hermogenes and Philetus.
Philetus was converted by the preaching of James, and
told Hermogenes that he was leaving him. Hermogenes
bound him fast by magical incantations, but Philetus
succeeded in sending word of his plight to James.
James sent back his kerchief and by its influence Philetus was freed. Hermogenes sent devils to fetch James

and Philetus, but they were powerless "to touch so much as an ant in his chamber." James sent the devils back to bring Hermogenes bound, which they did. When Hermogenes had been confounded, James bade Philetus to release him from his bonds. "Go free," said James, "for we do not render evil for evil." Hermogenes went home and destroyed all his magical books and returned to James and asked for pardon. "James sent him to undo his former work on those whom he had deceived, and to spend in charity what he had gained by his art. He obeyed and so grew in faith that he too performed miracles." (*The Apostolic History,* 4, 1-9.)

We have told this curious and fantastic story because the characters in it are connected with the strangest of all legends about James. To this day James is the patron saint of Spain. The connection of James with Spain is related thus. James, it is said, went to Spain and preached Christ to that country. He returned to Palestine and there he was executed by Herod. After the execution Hermogenes and Philetus embarked with James's body on a ship at Joppa. They slept and when they awoke next morning the ship was off the coast of Spain. There they came to land at a place called Iria Flavia, today called El Padron. For some time James's body lay there, and the most wonderful miracles happened through its influence. The body was lost in the eighth-century barbarian invasions of Spain. It was rediscovered in the ninth century and taken by King Alphonso the Chaste to Compostella, where, so it is said, it still lies. The name Compostella is in fact a corruption of either the Latin phrase *Ad Sanctum Jacobum Apostolum,* or the Spanish phrase, *Giacomo Postolo,* James the Apostle. To this day there is an image of the Virgin in Saragossa in Spain before which a hundred lamps are kept ever burning, for, it is said, when James was in Spain the Virgin appeared to him to strengthen and to encourage him in his work.

This story seems to appear first in the works of Isi-

dore of Seville who wrote in the seventh century, and
he appears to confuse James the brother of John, and
James the brother of Jesus. He writes, "James, the son
of Zebedee and the brother of John, fourth in the order
of the apostles, wrote to the twelve tribes who are dis-
persed among the Gentiles [Jas. 1:1], and preached
the gospel to Spain and the peoples of the West." Quite
certainly James the brother of John was not the James
who wrote the Letter of James. Considering the early
date of his martyrdom the connection of James with
Spain is impossible, however much we would wish it to
be true, and the whole story is one of the unexplained
mysteries of legend. In art James is depicted with a
copy of the gospels in one hand and a pilgrim staff and
scrip in the other, to show symbolically how far-trav-
elled an evangelist he was.

Even from this shadowy picture James emerges as a
man of certain definite characteristics.

1. Clearly James was a man of both courage and
forgiveness. The one definitely known fact about him
was that he was the first apostle to become a martyr,
and the one reasonably attested tradition about him is
that his courage and his forgiveness won even his pros-
ecutor for the Christian faith.

2. Equally clearly James was a man without jealousy. As Andrew lived in the shadow of Peter, so James
lived in the shadow of John. It can have been no easy
situation to have to live as the undistinguished relation
of a famous brother, but it was a situation from which
James triumphantly emerged.

3. It is clear that both James and John were men of
quite extraordinary faith. When they came with their
request to Jesus for the first places in his kingdom
(Matt. 20:20-28; Mark 10:33-45), they are usually
taken to be examples of worldly ambition, but that very
incident shows them as examples of divine optimism
and victorious faith. At that time nothing seemed less
likely than that Jesus would ever sit on any throne. He
was a homeless Galilean preacher following a course

which was bound to end in collision with the power of
the authorities and in inevitable disaster, and yet even
in that apparently hopeless situation, James and John
never doubted that Jesus Christ was a king.

4. But the most interesting thing of all emerges
when we put James and John together. On the occasion
when they asked for the chief places in his kingdom,
Jesus asked them if they could drink the cup which he
had to drink; they said that they could; and Jesus said
that the time would come when indeed they would
(Matt. 20:22-23; Mark 10:35-39). So, then, both of
the brothers drank the cup of Christ. Let us see what
that cup was. John went to Ephesus; he lived for almost a hundred years and died in peace, full of years
and honor. James's life was short and came to an end
swiftly and suddenly through martyrdom by the sword
—and yet both drank the cup of Christ. There is a
Roman coin which has as its inscription the picture of
an ox facing an altar and a plough with the words
"Ready for either." The ox must be ready for the dramatic sacrifice of the altar or the long routine of the
plough. The Christian who dies in one heroic moment,
and the Christian who lives a long life of fidelity to
Christ both drink the cup of Christ. The one is not the
superior of the other; they both have drunk the cup of
the Lord; the Christian too must be ready for either.

12

BARTHOLOMEW

Hitherto it has been my custom to place at the head of each chapter a descriptive sentence about the apostle with whom I was dealing. In the case of Bartholomew that is impossible, because, apart from his name, the New Testament tells us nothing whatever about him. It may well be that Bartholomew and Nathanael are to be identified as the same person; but, in order not to prejudge the case, we must deal with them separately.

Bartholomew's name occurs in every list of The Twelve (Matt. 10:3; Mark 3:18; Luke 6:14; Acts 1:13). When we were discussing the composition of the apostolic band, we already set down the reason for thinking that Bartholomew and Nathanael may well be different names for the same person; but let us here briefly recapitulate them.

1. Bartholomew is not itself a first name. It is a distinguishing second name, belonging to that class of second names which identifies a man by the name of his father. Bar means son of, Bartholomew probably means son of Tolmai. Bartholomew must, therefore, have had a first name; and, therefore, from the point of view of the difference of the names, there is nothing to forbid the identification of Bartholomew and Nathanael.

2. The first three Gospels never mention Nathanael, and the Fourth Gospel never mentions Bartholomew. The probability is that Nathanael was an apostle, although there are those who have questioned this. Certainly in the two passages where Nathanael is mentioned in the Fourth Gospel he is in the company of apostles and is spoken of in a way that makes it very likely that he was an apostle (John 1:43-51; 21:2). If

Bartholomew and Nathanael are both names within the twelve, then they must refer to the same person.

3. In the lists of the twelve in the first three Gospels and in Acts the names of Philip and Bartholomew always occur together, as if it was natural to speak of them together; and in the Fourth Gospel we learn that it was Philip who brought Nathanael to Jesus (John 1:45). Since, then, Philip is closely connected with Bartholomew and Nathanael, it may well be that Bartholomew and Nathanael are the same person.

The proof of the identity of Bartholomew and Nathanael falls short of certainty, and, as we shall see, Nathanael has been identified with many other people in the Gospel story; but nonetheless the converging lines of evidence make the identification of Bartholomew and Nathanael at least possible, and even probable. We shall, however, assemble the material about them separately.

Since the New Testament itself has nothing to tell us about Bartholomew, we must see what tradition and legend have to say about him.

By far the most interesting conjecture comes from Jerome. Jerome passes on the suggestion that Bartholomew was the only one of the twelve to be of noble birth. As we have seen, his name means son of Tolmai, or possibly son of Talmai. Now in II Sam. 3:3 there is mention of a Talmai who was king of Geshur; this Talmai had a daughter called Maacah; and this Maacah became the mother of Absalom, whom she bore to David. The suggestion is that it was from this Talmai that Bartholomew was descended, and that, therefore, he was of nothing less than royal lineage. Later still another story arose. The second part of Bartholomew's name was connected with Ptolemy, and he was said to be called son of Ptolemy. The Ptolemies were the kings of Egypt, and it was said that Bartholomew was connected with the royal house of Egypt. It cannot be said that these suggestions are really likely, but it would be of the greatest interest if in the apostolic band one who was of royal lineage lived in perfect fellowship with the humble fishermen of Galilee.

Many legends gather round the name of Bartholomew. These legends center round three spheres where Bartholomew was said to have preached the gospel.

He is said to have preached in India. Both Eusebius and Jerome pass on a story which connected Bartholomew with India (Eusebius, *The Ecclesiastical History,* 5, 10, 3; Jerome, *Concerning Illustrious Men,* 36). There was a famous stoic philosopher of Alexandria called Pantaenus, who was converted to the Christian faith. He went to preach the gospel in far off India. There he found people who were already Christian, and who possessed the Gospel of Matthew in the Hebrew language. "For Bartholomew, one of the apostles, had preached to them, and left them with the writing of Matthew in the Hebrew language, which they had preserved till that time." But, much as we would like to believe in it, we must regard Bartholomew's mission to India as, to say the least of it, doubtful.

He is said to have preached in Phrygia. We have already seen how the Acts of Philip tell how Philip and Bartholomew preached in Hierapolis and how Philip was martyred there by being pierced through the thighs and hung upside down. The story is that Bartholomew shared that campaign, escaped martyrdom, and lived to preach in other places.

He is said to have preached in Armenia, and the Armenian Church claims him as its founder. He is said to have been martyred at Albana, which is the modern Derbend. There is an account of the martyrdom of Bartholomew in *The Apostolic History* of Abdias, although there the death of Bartholomew seems to be located in India. The story runs as follows. Bartholomew preached with such success that the heathen gods were rendered powerless. A very interesting personal description of him is given.

He has black, curly hair, white skin, large eyes,

straight nose, his hair covers his ears, his beard long
and grizzled, middle height. He wears a white robe
with a purple stripe, and a white cloak with four
purple gems at the corners. For twenty-six years he
has worn these, and they never grow old. His shoes
have lasted twenty-six years. He prays a hundred
times a day and a hundred times a night. His voice is
like a trumpet; angels wait upon him; he is always
cheerful, and knows all languages.

Bartholomew did many wonderful things there, including the healing of the lunatic daughter of the king,
the exposing of the emptiness of the king's idol, and the
banishing of the demon who inhabited it. The demon
was visibly banished from the idol by an angel and
there is an interesting description of him—"black,
sharp-faced, with a long beard, hair to the feet, fiery
eyes, breathing flame, and spiky wings like a hedge-
hog."

The king and many others were baptized; but the
priests remained hostile. The priests went to the king's
brother Astyages. The king's brother had Bartholomew
arrested, beaten with clubs, flayed alive, and crucified
in agony. And so Bartholomew died a martyr for his
Lord.

There is still extant an apocryphal Gospel of Bartholomew which Jerome knew. It describes a series of
questions which Bartholomew addressed to Jesus and
to Mary in the time between the Resurrection and the
Ascension. Four questions are asked.

Bartholomew asks Jesus whither he went from the
cross. Jesus' answer is that he went down to the house
of Hades, scourged Hades himself, and bound him in
chains that cannot be loosed, "and brought forth thence
all the patriarchs and came again unto the Cross." That
is a very interesting and very early interpretation of the
meaning of "The Descent into Hell."

Bartholomew then asks questions about how many
souls die and are born each day. The figures vary in

different Manuscripts; but the answer is that thirty
thousand souls die each day, of whom only three are
found righteous; and thirty thousand and one souls are
born each day into the world.

Bartholomew then asks Mary about the Annuncia-
tion, and Mary describes her experience. One of the
features of the Gospel of Bartholomew is the splendor
of the prayers which it contains. Before Mary tells of
her experience, she prays, and this is her address to
God:

> O God, the exceeding great and all-wise, king of
> the worlds, thou art not to be described, the ineffa-
> ble, that didst establish the greatness of the heavens
> and all things by a word, that out of darkness didst
> constitute and fasten together the poles of heaven in
> harmony, didst bring into shape the matter that was
> in confusion, didst bring into order the things that
> were without order, didst part the misty darkness
> from the light, didst establish in one place the foun-
> dation of the waters, thou that makest the beings of
> the air to tremble and art the fear of them that are
> on the earth, and didst settle the earth and not suffer
> it to perish, and filledst it, which is the nourisher of
> all things, with showers of blessing.

Bartholomew then asks to see the abyss and the adversary of man. Beliar is then revealed to him, and
Bartholomew is permitted to place his foot upon his
neck.

At the end of the Gospel there is an interesting interpretation of the sin against the Holy Spirit. Bartholomew asks Jesus what that sin is, and Jesus' answer is:
"Whosoever shall decree against any man that hath
served my Holy Father hath blasphemed against the
Holy Spirit. For every man that serveth God worship-
fully is worthy of the Holy Spirit, and he that speaketh
anything evil against him shall not be forgiven." Those
who were spreading the gospel felt that those who op-

posed the gospel were guilty of a sin than which none could be heavier.

At the end of his questioning Bartholomew "took hold of the hand of the Lord the lover of men," and uttered a magnificent ascription of praise:

> Glory be to Thee, O Lord Jesus Christ, that givest unto all the grace that all we have perceived. Alleluia.
> Glory be to Thee, O Lord, the life of sinners.
> Glory be to Thee, O Lord, death is put to shame.
> Glory be to Thee, O Lord, the treasure of righteousness.
> For unto God do we sing.

No doubt the Gospel of Bartholomew is only a pious fiction, but it was certainly written by someone who had seen the glory of God.

The New Testament tells us nothing about Bartholomew except his name, but the later stories—and they are at least true in spirit—tell us of a man who intimately knew his Lord, who lived and preached and died for the faith.

13

NATHANAEL

Our knowledge of Nathanael comes from two passages in the Fourth Gospel. Nathanael came from Cana in Galilee (John 21:2). He was a friend of Philip, and when Philip discovered Jesus he went straight to Nathanael and communicated his discovery to him. It was Philip's belief that in Jesus of Nazareth, the son of Joseph, he had discovered the Messiah to whom all the Law and the prophets pointed. Nathanael was skeptical —we shall see that there is another possible interpretation of Nathanael's attitude—and found it hard to believe that so great a figure could emerge from a place like Nazareth. It was not that Nazareth had a specially bad reputation, but Cana and Nazareth were to all intents and purposes neighboring villages and rivalry and familiarity had bred contempt. Philip did not waste time and breath in argument; he invited Nathanael to come and meet Jesus for himself. Jesus greeted Nathanael with the words: "Behold an Israelite indeed, in whom is no guile!" Nathanael asked how Jesus knew who he was. Jesus answered that before Philip had called him he had seen him under the fig tree.

The point of this saying is that for many people in Palestine the fig tree was a kind of private room. The fig tree grows to a height of about fifteen feet, but its branches have a spread of as much as twenty-five feet. It was the custom to have a fig tree at the door of the cottage. In Palestine the houses of the poorer people had only one room; and often, when they sought quietness to pray and to meditate, they sought privacy beneath the shade of the fig tree. In effect Jesus was saying to Nathanael, "Nathanael, I saw you at prayer, in your private devotion in the only secret place you have, there I saw into the secret and private places of your heart; and I know the seeking that is there." It is as if Jesus like God himself understood Nathanael's thought afar off. (See Ps. 139:2.) To Nathanael it seemed an amazing thing that anyone should have the divine power to read the secrets of his heart. "Rabbi," he said in awed amazement, "thou art the Son of God; thou art the King of Israel." Thereupon Jesus promised Nathanael even greater things; he promised him that he would be a witness of the ultimate triumph and glory of the end (John 1:43-51).

The figure of Nathanael has always exercised a kind of fascination over the minds of students of the New Testament. He has been identified with many people.

1. As we have already seen, he is very commonly identified with Bartholomew. That was not an identification that men were quick to make, for it would seem that the first man to make it was Elias of Damascus, a Nestorian of the ninth century.

2. He has been identified with Simon the Cananaean. As we have already seen, the inferior manuscripts of the New Testament call Simon by the name *Kananitēs*. That was wrongly taken by some to mean man of Cana. In John 21:2 we read that Nathanael also was a man of Cana, and so the identification was made. That identification cannot be possible, because Simon was not the man of Cana, but the Cananaean or Zealot.

3. Epiphanius, on what grounds we do not know, identified Nathanael with the unnamed disciple of the walk to Emmaus (Luke 24:13-25; *Heresies,* 23). In that scene one of the disciples whom Jesus met on the Emmaus road is called Cleopas, and the other remains anonymous. Epiphanius believed that the disciple without a name was Nathanael.

4. Nathanael has been identified with The Beloved Disciple, and therefore, with John himself. Jesus' first words to Nathanael were, "Behold an Israelite indeed, in whom is no guile" (John 1:47). It is as if Jesus said, "Here indeed is the perfect disciple for my purposes." It would not be difficult to believe that such a man

grew into The Beloved Disciple as the days passed in the company of Jesus.

5. Most interesting and most ingenious is the identification of Nathanael with Stephen. The basis of that suggestion is that Jesus promised Nathanael that he would see the heavens open, and the angels of God ascending and descending upon the Son of Man (John 1:51). When Stephen was martyred, it is said of him that he saw the heavens opened and Jesus standing on the right hand of God (Acts 7:56). It is said that Stephen inherited the very promise made to Nathanael, and so they are identified.

Interesting and ingenious though these other suggestions are, if Nathanael is to be identified with anyone in the apostolic company, it must be with Bartholomew.'

We must note that certain of the greatest of the early fathers did not think that Nathanael was one of the twelve at all. Their reason was that they believed Nathanael to be a very great expert and scholar in the Law and the prophets. To this day the Roman Catholic scholars speak of Nathanael as a "doctor in the law." Augustine, for instance, believed that it was for that very reason that Nathanael was not a member of the apostolic twelve, because Jesus sought to change the world with the help only of unlearned men (*Homilies on John*, 7). Gregory the Great shared that view. The first words which Jesus spoke to Nathanael were words of praise; he called him an Israelite in whom there is no guile. For that very reason, said Gregory, Nathanael was passed over as a member of the twelve, for Jesus wished to show by the choice of apostles who had nothing praiseworthy of their own, that their sufficiency came, not from themselves, but from God (Gregory the Great, *Mor.*, 33).

Where did they get this idea that Nathanael was a great scholar and a "doctor in the law"? Nathanael's answer to Philip's announcement of the discovery of Jesus appears in almost every translation in the form of a question: "Can there any good thing come out of

Nazareth?" (John 1:46). In the early Greek manuscripts there is no punctuation, and it is theoretically possible that the words of Nathanael are not a question, but a statement. Augustine says: "Nathanael, who knew the Scriptures excellently well, when he heard the name of Nazareth, was filled with hope and said, 'From Nazareth something good can come.' " Some few have believed that when Nathanael heard the news which Philip brought, he said meditatively, "Yes, you may be right; for out of Nazareth something good may come."

Why should that make Nathanael so great a scholar in the Law and the prophets? Matthew has a saying concerning the coming of Jesus to Nazareth: "And he came and dwelt in a city called Nazareth; that it might be fulfilled which was spoken by the prophets, He shall be called a Nazarene" (Matt. 2:23). That saying of Matthew is one of the mysteries of biblical quotation, for no one has ever been able satisfactorily to identify the prophecy which Matthew was quoting. The idea is that Nathanael was such an expert in the Law and the prophets that he alone could identify the prophecy which no one else has ever been able to identify.

That is ingenious and interesting and attractive, but the fact remains that by far the more natural interpretation of the Greek of Nathanael's words is that they were a question, springing from contempt for the village of Nazareth which he knew so well.

Meager as our information about Nathanael is, it is nonetheless true that when we put it together the character of Nathanael clearly emerges.

1. Nathanael was a searcher of the scriptures and a seeker after truth. The way in which Philip put his announcement is the proof of that: "We have found him, of whom Moses in the law, and the prophets, did write" (John 1:45). The clear implication is that Philip and Nathanael have spent long hours poring over the words of scripture, searching for information as to what the Messiah must be like and as to when he

should come. It was because Philip and Nathanael sought for truth and studied the word of God that they were able to recognize the Son of God when he came.

2. Nathanael was a man of complete sincerity. He was an Israelite indeed in whom there was no guile (John 1:47). The proof of that is his willingness to be convinced. At first he was unwilling to believe that any good thing could come out of Nazareth, but when he was confronted with Jesus, his prejudices and his pre-suppositions vanished, and he believed. Plummer describes Nathanael as "a good man, hampered by preju-dice, but quite willing to be enlightened." There are those who will not see anything except what they wish to see, but Nathanael had that sincerity which enabled him to recognize the truth, even when it contradicted all his preconceived ideas.

3. Nathanael was a man of prayer. It was under the fig tree that Jesus saw him (John 1:48). The implica-tion of the story is that Nathanael spent many an hour there. To his study Nathanael added prayer. And when the light of study is warmed by the fire of devotion, then indeed discoveries are made.

4. Nathanael was a man who knew no half mea-sures. "Thou art the Son of God," he said to Jesus, "thou art the King of Israel" (John 1:49). When Nathanael surrendered, he surrendered completely. When he discovered Jesus Christ, none but the highest place was good enough for him.

5. Nathanael was a man of staying power. He was still there with the apostles after the agony of the Cross (John 21:2). "Thou art the King of Israel," he had said. The man whom he called king found a cross for his throne, but Nathanael still believed.

If we may identify Nathanael and Bartholomew, we can see in the composite picture one of the completest characters in the New Testament. The resulting figure is the figure of a man who was a seeking student, a man who was earnest in prayer, a man who made the complete surrender, and a man who became a man of action and one of the most adventurous missionaries in the history of the Church.

14

JAMES, THE SON OF ALPHAEUS

James, the son of Alphaeus, is the apostle about whom we know least. The New Testament tells us nothing but his name (Matt. 10:3; Mark 3:18; Luke 6:15; Acts 1:13), and even legend and tradition are almost silent about him. The only things that legend says about him are that he preached in Persia, and that he died a martyr by crucifixion. When we study closely all that the New Testament says and implies about this James, we may come to three conclusions, of which one is almost certainly fact, one a reasonable deduction, and one conjecture.

1. James is identified as the son of Alphaeus. The first three Gospels all tell us about the call of Matthew (Matt. 9:9; Mark 2:14; Luke 5:27, 28). For our present purposes it is the accounts of Matthew and Mark which are most significant. Matthew says: "And as Jesus passed forth from thence, he saw a man, named Matthew, sitting at the receipt of custom: and he saith unto him, Follow me." Mark says: "And as he passed by, he saw Levi the son of Alphaeus sitting at the receipt of custom, and said unto him, Follow me." There is no doubt that Matthew and Levi are the same person. Since that is so, the name of Matthew's father was also Alphaeus; and Matthew and this James must have been brothers.

2. In the lists of Matthew and Mark the last four apostles to be named are James the son of Alphaeus, Thaddaeus, Simon the Zealot, and Judas Iscariot (Matt. 10:3-4; Mark 3:18-19). In Luke's lists the last four disciples are James the son of Alphaeus, Simon Zēlōtēs, Judas the brother of James and Judas Iscariot (6:15-16; Acts 1:13). It is all but certain that Judas the brother of James and Thaddaeus are the same person.

Since these four are so consistently named together, there must have been some common factor which bound them into a group. Simon, we know, was a Zealot, a fanatical Jewish patriot; Judas Iscariot, it is probable, was also such a patriot. One important Latin manuscript calls Judas the brother of James, Judas the Zealot. In *The Apostolic Constitutions*, which purport to give the regulations which each of the apostles contributed to the administration and structure of the Church, Thaddaeus is credited with the regulations concerning widows. In two of the ancient Manuscripts of that work there is a note describing Thaddaeus thus, "Thaddaeus, also called Lebbaeus, who was surnamed Judas the Zealot." There is thus a considerable amount of evidence that Thaddaeus was also a Zealot. So then, Simon, Thaddaeus or Judas, and Judas Iscariot were all most probably Zealots. It must, then, be a reasonable deduction that the fourth member of this unaltering group shared the sympathies of the other three. It must be regarded as extremely probable that James, the son of Alphaeus, Simon the Zealot, Thaddaeus or Judas, and Judas Iscariot were bound together by the bond of intense and fanatical patriotism, and may well all four have once belonged to the Zealot party.

3. So we have our fact and our reasonable deduction. Matthew and James the son of Alphaeus were brothers. James was very probably a Jewish nationalist of the most fiery type, and both were members of the apostolic company. Is it possible to see here a great reconciliation? Here were two brothers who drifted further and further apart. Matthew entered the service of Herod Antipas and became a tax collector in an administration that was subject to Rome. James became a Zealot with a flaming patriotism and an embittered hatred of all who in the least degree compromised with Rome. Is it not likely that the brothers Matthew and James, once brought up in the same home, came to a situation in which they hated each other, a situation in which James regarded Matthew as a renegade traitor, a

situation in which James would have plunged his dagger into Matthew? Then Jesus came, and Jesus called both of them, and in the presence of this common Master the brothers who had drifted apart came together again; the brothers who had hated each other were reconciled.

It may well be that the fact that Matthew and James were both members of the twelve is one of the great illustrations that Jesus came not only to reconcile men to God but also to reconcile them to each other.

15

THADDAEUS

Jerome called Thaddaeus Trinomius, which means the man with three names. In Mark he is called Thaddaeus (3:18); in Matthew he is called Lebbaeus whose surname was Thaddaeus (10:3); in Luke he is called Judas the brother of James (Luke 6:16; Acts 1:13).

We have already dealt in our opening chapter with the identification of Thaddaeus and Judas the son of James, and we may regard it as certain.

In the first three Gospels no word or action of Thaddaeus is recorded, but in the Fourth Gospel he makes one appearance under the name Judas, not Iscariot. At the Last Supper he has one question to ask, "Lord, how is it that thou wilt manifest thyself unto us, and not unto the world?" And Jesus gave him the answer, "If a man love me, he will keep my words: and my Father will love him, and we will come unto him, and make our abode with him" (John 14:22-23). What is the point and meaning of this interchange between Judas and Jesus? In our last chapter we saw that in one Latin manuscript this Judas is called Judas the Zealot. We have seen that most likely Judas or Thaddaeus was an intense and violent nationalist with the dream of world power and dominion for the chosen people. Because of that, as the days drew to their now inevitable close, he could not understand Jesus. What he is saying is: "It is all very well to tell us that you are the Messiah, and to show us that you are the Chosen One of God. But surely the time has come when a public manifestation is necessary. Surely the time has come when you must go out to the people and show them who you are and demonstrate your power." Jesus answer was that any manifestation of himself was impossible except to the obedient and the loving heart,

but that when a man did give Jesus love and obedience
the Father and the Son would make the heart of that
man their dwelling place and their abode. Thaddaeus
was telling Jesus to go out to the crowds of strangers
and to dazzle, and if need be, to blast, them into loyalty. And Jesus was telling Thaddaeus that the only
loyalty which was of any use to him was the loyalty of
the loving heart and the surrendered life. Jesus was
telling Thaddaeus the nationalist that the way of power
can never be a substitute for the way of love.

The name of Thaddaeus is connected with one of the
most romantic and attractive legends of the early
Church, which has come down to us in the works of
both Eusebius and Jerome amongst others (Eusebius,
The Ecclesiastical History, 1, 13; Jerome, *Homily on
Matthew,* 10, 4). This legend tells of a correspondence
between Jesus and Abgarus, King of Edessa, which was
a city in Northern Mesopotamia near the Euphrates.
Eusebius claims to have seen this correspondence in
the archives and public registers of Edessa and to have
translated it himself from the Syriac language. The
correspondence begins with a letter from Abgarus to
Jesus, headed, "Copy of a letter written by Abgarus the
ruler to Jesus, and sent to him at Jerusalem by Ananias
the swift courier." The letter runs:

Abgarus, ruler of Edessa, to Jesus the excellent
Saviour who has appeared in the country of Jerusalem, greeting. I have heard the reports of thee and of
thy cures as performed by thee without medicine and
without herbs. For it is said that thou makest the
blind to see and the lame to walk, that thou cleansest
lepers and casteth out impure spirits and demons,
and that thou healest those afflicted with lingering
disease, and raisest the dead. And having heard all
these things concerning thee, I have concluded that
one of two things must be true: either, thou art God,
and having come down from heaven thou doest these
things or else, thou who doest these things art the

Son of God. I have therefore written to thee to ask
thee that thou wouldst take the trouble to come to
me and heal the disease which I have. For I have
heard that the Jews are murmuring against thee and
are plotting to injure thee. But I have a very small
yet noble city which is big enough for us both.

The reply is headed, "The answer of Jesus to the ruler
Abgarus by the courier Ananias." The reply runs:

> Blessed art thou who hast believed in me without
> having seen me. For it is written concerning me that
> they who have seen me will not believe in me, and
> that they who have not seen me will believe and be
> saved. But in regard to what thou hast written to me,
> that I should come to thee, it is necessary for me to
> fulfil all things here for which I have been sent, and
> after I have fulfilled them thus to be taken up again
> to him that sent me. But after I have been taken up I
> will send to thee one of my disciples, that he may
> heal thy disease, and give life to thee and to thine.

The story goes on to tell that after the Ascension of
Jesus, Thomas sent Thaddaeus—here called "an apostle and one of the seventy"—to Edessa. Thaddaeus
took up his residence with a man called Tobias. He
healed so many that report of him came to Abgarus,
and Abgarus knew that Thaddaeus was the one whom
Jesus had promised to send. He sent for Thaddaeus.
Thaddaeus told him: "Because thou hast mightily believed in him that sent me, therefore have I been sent
unto thee. And still further, if thou believest in him, the
petitions of thy heart shall be granted thee, as thou believest." "So much have I believed in him," said Abgarus, "that I wished to take an army and destroy those
Jews who crucified him, if I had not been deterred
from it by reason of the dominion of the Romans." So
Thaddaeus healed him and many another. Abgarus
then asked Thaddaeus to tell him all things about

Jesus. Thaddaeus asked him on the morrow to assemble all the citizens, and he would tell them all. Thaddaeus' summary of his own message is of the greatest interest, because even if the whole story is a beautiful fiction, it nonetheless enables us to see the basic missionary message of the early preachers.

I will preach in their presence, and sow among them the word of God, concerning the coming of Jesus, how he was born; and concerning his mission, for what purpose he was sent by the Father; and concerning the power of his works, and the mysteries which he proclaimed in the world, and by what power he did these things; and concerning his new preaching, and his abasement and humiliation, and how he humbled himself, and died and debased his divinity and was crucified, and descended into Hades, and burst the bars which from eternity had not been broken, and raised the dead; for he descended alone and rose with many, and thus ascended to his Father.

So the story ends that Abgarus offered Thaddaeus much gold and silver, but Thaddaeus would not take them. "If we have forsaken that which is our own, how shall we take that which is another's?"

It is of interest to see how a legend can grow more and more elaborate. The later form of the legend is that when Jesus could not himself go to Edessa he allowed Ananias to try to paint a picture of him to satisfy the longing of Abgarus to see him. Ananias could not paint for the light and glory which flowed from the face of Jesus. So Jesus drew a garment over his face, and on the garment the picture of his face was left, and so the garment was sent to Abgarus, and became the means whereby many miracles were wrought (John of Damascus, *The Exposition of the Orthodox Faith*, 4, 16).

It is then said that Thaddaeus went on to preach the

gospel in other places, and that finally he was killed with arrows at Ararat.

The legend of Abgarus and Thaddaeus is a lovely legend, and with it we may well end, for the task of Thaddaeus was the task of all the apostles—first, to live with Jesus, and then, to take to men the light and the healing which Jesus brought to all the world.

LIST OF SOURCES

The primary source for the lives of the apostles is of course none other than the New Testament itself. The great Bible dictionaries summarize the biblical material and indicate to some extent the legendary material. The main dictionaries are:

Cheyne, T. K. and Black, J. Sutherland. (eds.). *Encyclopedia Biblica*. New York: The Macmillan Company, 1899.

Cross, F. L. (ed.). *The Oxford Dictionary of the Christian Church*. New York: Oxford University Press, 1957.

Hastings, James and Selbie, J. A. (eds.). *A Dictionary of Christ and the Gospels*. 2 vols. New York: Charles Scribner's Sons, 1906-8.

Hastings, James; Selbie, J. A.; and Lambert, J. D. (eds.). *Dictionary of the Apostolic Church*. 2 vols. New York: Charles Scribner's Sons, 1916.

Hastings, James *et al*. (eds.). *Dictionary of the Bible*. New York: Charles Scribner's Sons, 1927.

Smith, William and Cheetham, Samuel. (eds). *Dictionary of Christian Antiquities*.

Smith, William and Wace, Henry. (eds.). *Dictionary of Christian Biography*. 4 vols. Boston: Little, Brown and Company, 1877-87.

There is a good deal of scattered material in the early church historians, and in certain of the early fathers. The main material is in the following works:

Eusebius. *The Church History*. There is a Greek text and translation by Kirsopp Lake in the Loeb

Classical Library. New York: William Heinemann
Ltd., 1929. There is an excellent translation with
prolegomena and notes by Arthur C. McGiffert in
*A Select Library of Nicene and Post-Nicene Fa-
thers of the Christian Church.* Second series, vol.
I. Grand Rapids, Mich.: William B. Eerdmans
Publishing Company, 1952.

The same series contains the following works:

Cassian, John. *The Conferences,* tr. Edgar C. S.
Gibson. Vol. XI, 1955.
Jerome. *The Lives of Illustrious Men,* tr. Ernest C.
Richardson. Vol. III, 1953.
Salaminius Hermias Sozomen. *The Ecclesiastical
History,* tr. Chester D. Hartranft. Vol. II, 1952.
Socrates Scholasticus. *The Ecclesiastical History,* tr.
A. C. Zenos. Vol. II, 1952.

Irenaeus' *Against Heresies* is translated in the *Ante-
Nicene Christian Library* by A. Roberts and W. H.
Rambaut. *The Rich Man's Salvation* is translated by G.
W. Butterworth in the volume of Clement of Alexan-
dria's works in the Loeb Classical Library.

There is a vast amount of material, of course quite
uncritical and often obviously legendary and unhistori-
cal, in the great works on the lives of the saints. Of
these works two may be cited:

Butler, Alban. *Lives of the Fathers, Martyrs and
Other Principal Saints.* London: Virtue and Com-
pany Ltd., 1949.
Gould, S. Baring. *Lives of the Saints.*

The legendary and apocryphal material on the lives
and acts of the apostles is to be found in Montague
Rhodes James's invaluable *The Apocryphal New Testament.* New York: Oxford University Press, 1924. In-
cluded in that collection are "The Gospel According to

the Hebrews," "The Arabic Gospel of the Infancy," "The Protevangelium" or "The Book of James," "The Gospel of Peter," "The Gospel of Bartholomew," "The Acts of John," "The Acts of Peter," "The Acts of Andrew," "The Acts of Thomas," "The Acts of Andrew and Matthias" (Matthew), "The Martyrdom of Matthew," "The Apostolic History of Pseudo-Abdias," "The Acts of Thaddaeus," and "The Letters of Christ and Abgarus."

The most convenient summary of the connection of Thomas with India is to be found in the article by Robert Sinker in the *Dictionary of Christian Antiquities.*

The material on the connection of Andrew with Scotland will be found in the *Aberdeen Breviary, the Chronicle of the Picts and Scots* and in the Bollandist *Acts of the Martyrs,* where it is found under October 17 in connection with Regulus. It is evaluated in Skene's *Celtic Scotland.* A convenient summary of it is to be found in *Lives and Legends of Apostles and Evangelists,* by Myrtle Strode-Jackson.

Experience more of the richness of the Scriptures from this legendary expositor in

William Barclay's

Introducing the Bible

"William Barclay testifies to the Bible's uniqueness, gives clear advice on how best to read it, tells how the biblical writings came into being and finally gained acceptance as Scripture, and explains the significance and status of the Apocrypha."

—Christianity Today

"This informative little book will make the Bible one of the most exciting challenges life can offer."

—Interpreter

"Helpful guides for conducting a Bible study. Especially good for the young Christian."

—Christianity Today

"Barclay is incapable of boring; he is a joyous Christian and his sense of fun shines through his writings."

—Clift Rodgers Library

"A handy paperback which will whet your appetite to tackle the entire Bible."

—Christian Herald